God, Are You *Really* There?

Don England

21ST CENTURY CHRISTIAN

2809 Granny White Pike • Nashville, TN 37204

All Scripture citations are from the Revised Standard Version unless
otherwise indicated.

Contents

FOREWORD

Dr. Don England has performed a generous service to Christians of all ages in this work. He writes as both an honest scientist and as a dedicated believer in the Lord Jesus Christ.

He is careful to note the nature of evidence that is used in the scientific disciplines and the nature of evidence that is necessary to examine the claims of Christianity.

Dr. England provides a calm, steady defense of the Christian faith that is appealing to the believer and thought provoking to the one who is searching for answers to some very nagging and inevitable problems.

Our century has witnessed the result of the denial of the Bible in 18th century thought and the rejection of God from many of the 19th century philosophers. The fact that more have been killed in this century by war than in all of the preceding centuries combined declares the need of a reexamination of the secularism that has denied the absolutes in morality while reducing man to the animal level.

This work by a mature Christian thinker will serve as a valuable reference for the Christian's home library. It also deserves to be made available on a large scale to the general reading public. Congregations would do well to use this book in evangelistic efforts.

As I think back over nearly forty years of lecturing to college and high-school students in Africa, Asia, Europe as well as throughout the United States concerning reasons for Christian belief, I am certain that you will join with me in expressing to Dr. England a sincere word of thanks for his work.

Virgil R. Trout
7 March 1989

ACKNOWLEDGMENTS

I gratefully acknowledge the encouragement and assistance of numerous persons in the completion of this book. The initial suggestion for the project came from Dr. David Burks, President of Harding University. Tom Eddins, Associate Professor of Bible, provided many hours of enjoyable dialogue as a capable resource person. Tom also carefully read the entire manuscript and made many valuable suggestions. Dr. Neale Pryor, Vice President for Academic Affairs and Professor of Bible, and Dr. Rubel Shelly, pulpit minister for the Woodmont Hills congregation, Nashville, Tennessee, critiqued the entire manuscript as did also David Crouch, Director of Public Relations, and Tim Bruner, Director of Alumni Relations. Dr. James Mackey, Professor of Physics, and Dr. Michael Plummer, Professor of Biology, Harding University, read portions of the manuscript pertinent to their areas of expertise.

My wife, Lynn, to whom I lovingly dedicate this book, helped beyond measure in a word-by-word evaluation of the text. Also reading the manuscript and offering valuable suggestions were Sherry Organ and Beth Van Rheenen. I also express gratitude to Mr. Bob Niebel, Sr. and the staff of 21st Century Christian, Nashville, Tennessee.

I would like to credit everyone from whom ideas expressed on the following pages have been gathered over the years. That, however, is impossible. I do wish to acknowledge my colleagues, Drs. Harmon Brown, James Mackey, and Jack Sears; the students of Physical Science 410; and the last three pulpit ministers of the College congregation, Searcy, Arkansas: Mike Cope, Dale Foster, and James Woodroof. These persons, over several years, have provided mental stimulation in the areas covered in this book, which is sent forth with the prayer and expectation that Christian faith will be triumphant in the lives of those who consider it.

Don England

Keep Thou my feet;
I do not ask to see the distant scene—
One step enough for me.
                    J.H. Newman

1

Is Seeing
Better Than Believing?

Brian had just celebrated his 18th birthday. Tonight he was in a particularly reflective mood as he thought about high school graduation, armed services registration, college, and, of particular concern, the distressing feeling that life seems unfair. Life is unfair— because a teen-age girl whom he knew to be a lovely Christian person had recently been injured in a head-on collision with a drunken driver, and she was not expected to live.

Not saying anything to other members of the family, Brian stepped onto the patio, walked to a dark corner, looked up at a particularly bright star, and began to wonder, "God, are you *really* there?"

As far back as Brian could remember, his parents had been teaching him about God. He was now having nagging, doubtful thoughts, and that was very troubling. In fact, he was a bit ashamed and embarrassed for even having these thoughts. He knew his parents and his Bible class teacher would not approve. However, a science teacher at school whom Brian greatly admired had recently told his biology class there was no need to believe in God because modern science is answering all of our questions.

Many of Brian's friends, especially those whom he knew through the church, seemed to have no difficulty believing, but he also knew that some of the students at school did not believe in God. Equally disturbing was the fact that several of his friends, even some who "went to church" with their parents, did things of which God would clearly disapprove. Brian tried to push all of these thoughts out of

1

his mind, but he knew that he could not. He knew that he was going to have to confront some tough issues.

The thoughts of college next year were also disturbing. Several of Brian's close Christian friends who had graduated last year had gone to State U. Some of them had confided to him that the only time they now "go to church" is when they are home with their parents; it is just not the thing to do with the new friends they now have at the university. Brian knew that it did not have to be that way with him, but he was afraid that it might be.

On the other hand, he knew that he could go to a Christian college or university where he hoped that his faith would grow stronger. It was then Brian realized that, for the first time, he had used the word *faith* as he thought about these things. The stars had grown brighter as he stood there. Slowly Brian began to realize that whether he went to State U. or a Christian college he was going to have to get a better grip on the meaning of the word, *faith*.

Brian is not alone. Every young person of sensitive conscience has entertained many of the same thoughts, and it is safe to say that those who have managed to escape Brian's concerns should have faced them. Man is an incurably inquisitive being when it comes to wondering about such questions as "Does God exist?" "Has God spoken?" "Is the Bible really that spoken message?" "What about Jesus Christ—can he really be God and man?" "Is man anything more than an intelligent chimpanzee or ape?" and, the most bothersome question of all, "How can one reconcile the idea of the existence of God with the fact that Brian's lovely Christian friend was possibly going to die?"

What is Faith?

Many young people and adults are like Brian in our scientifically advanced age. They naturally wonder, "Can an intelligent person really believe in God?" They also wonder, "Can the Bible be trusted, or is it merely an accumulation of myths and superstitions? Does it make sense to believe in something that one cannot see or experience with the senses?" These are questions of faith, and faith is where we begin.

The word *faith* may be used in many different ways. To understand

2

the way in which the word is used in this book, consider the following illustration. An airplane is about to take off from San Francisco en route to Melbourne, Australia, via Honolulu, Hawaii. The pilot is experienced and has made the flight many times before. He has a rational faith in the aerodynamics of flight because of his previous flight experience, training, and knowledge. He has confidence in the voice that speaks to him from the control tower and in the radar beam that keeps him on course. Many of the passengers have flown before and have a rational faith in the pilot's experience and knowledge of the mechanics of flight.

Let us also suppose, however, that on this flight there is one passenger who has never flown before or even seen an airplane on or off of the ground. He has been told by a complete stranger that if he purchased a ticket and boarded the oblong craft with wheels and wings, he would arrive in Melbourne, Australia, in about fifteen hours. This passenger, on boarding the craft, does not observe that there is a cabin with pilots, yet he proceeds to take a comfortable seat, believing the words of the stranger he has just met. In contrast to the other passengers, this person has a nonrational faith as he begins his journey.

Both the informed passengers and the uninformed passenger have *faith*. However, the experienced passengers have a rational faith because it is based on knowledge, experience, and evidence. The uninformed passenger's faith is not based on evidence and is, therefore, nonrational. Clearly, one would expect the informed travelers to feel more secure on their journey.

Since Christianity is a religion which is based in historical evidence, it is rational. People who understand the basis for Christian faith, therefore, possess a rational faith. Unfortunately, some Christians are like the uninformed airplane passenger. They have never examined their faith. They have not bothered to investigate the evidence that shows Christianity to be rational. A Christian girl recently said to me, "I do not want to think about my faith." Tragedy awaits persons with this attitude.

Hebrews 11:1 is often cited as a biblical definition of *faith*. Rather than being a definition of faith, it would better be understood as a description of faith: "Now faith is the assurance of things hoped for, the conviction of things not seen." Assurance or conviction cannot be rational unless it is based on experience, knowledge, or

3

evidence. Christian faith is a way of looking at reality through the eyes of Jesus Christ. Because he trusts in God, the Christian believer perceives unseen realities as if they are seen realities (2 Corinthians 4:18).

Everyone Relies on Faith

There is no such thing as complete unbelief; *everyone* believes *something*. The farmer, banker, physician, teacher, student, philosopher, and scientist all rely on faith. The scientist has faith in the orderliness of nature and in his ability to correctly perceive nature. He believes in the existence of electrons, protons, and neutrons although he has never seen them. In the scientific process, the scientist relies upon faith but goes to great lengths to minimize its role. The scientist has no basis to ridicule the Christian for being a person of faith, and the Christian should not apologize to the scientist because he has faith.

Both science and Christianity rely on rational faith. However, a central difference between the two is that a scientist relies more on *sight* and less on faith. In fact, he often expends great effort to design new instruments to minimize faith. However, the scientist never quite eliminates faith. The Christian, on the other hand, cultivates, enhances, and nourishes faith so that he relies more on *faith* and less on sight (2 Corinthians 5:7).

It is unfortunate if a Christian reverses the biblical priority so that he walks by sight rather than by faith. You are cautioned about this early in our study because reversing the biblical priority is a major pitfall to be avoided in a study of Christian evidences. There is always the danger that a study of this nature will be misused to exclude faith rather than to emphasize that faith has a rational basis. Any use of the evidences of Christianity which does not draw one closer to Jesus Christ is an abuse. Evidences must show that Christianity is rational, but the evidences themselves are not the object of faith. Christ alone should be the object of a Christian's faith.

Concerning the existence of God, a study of this nature should show that faith in God makes sense, but it is inappropriate to attempt to prove God scientifically and eliminate a reliance on trust. We must always remember that God calls man on the basis of trusting faith and not on sight (Hebrews. 11:6). Likewise, in reference to the Bible, God's Word, it is proper to demonstrate reasons why we believe Scripture to be the inspired Word of God. It is inappropriate, however, to make the Bible something God never intended it to be: a book of science.

The New Testament was written at a time when the philosophical climate of the day was hostile to Christian faith. In many respects it is no different today. The Apostle Peter, in the following text, calls upon the Christian to be ready to make a logical or rational defense of his faith:

> Always be prepared to make a defense to any one who calls you to account for the hope that is in you, yet do it with gentleness and reverence. 1 Peter 3:15

To be able to do what Peter commands, we must know *what* we believe, but we must also know *why* we believe it. It is not easy to think through one's faith. The Christian, however, is commanded to do just that: he should be able to present clues, evidence, and indicators that point to the truthfulness of his faith. He should also take note that, when he is called upon to defend his faith, he should do so in the spirit of gentleness and reverence. Haughtiness and bitterness are never appropriate, especially when one is defending his faith in God.

Faith Must Result in Response

To many people, faith is nothing more than an intellectual assent to the existence of something which cannot be experienced by the senses. Indeed, faith is something like a sixth sense and, properly understood, is much more than intellectual assent. The biblical concept of faith goes beyond one's experience with the fragrant odor of a rose, the silky touch of its petals, and the symmetry of the flower to acknowledge its Designer and Creator. However, we are told in James 2:19 that even demons acknowledge God's existence. The difference is that the faith of demons does not evoke an obedient response; it merely causes them to tremble in disobedience.

As I recently taught a woman about Christ in a medical missions campaign in Kingston, Jamaica, she fought back tears saying, "I believe what I have been taught, and I want to become a Christian, but I cannot." When asked why, she responded, "I run a liquor store, and I cannot give up my business." A man with whom I studied said, "I believe everything I have been taught, but I cannot become a Christian because I will have to quit living in sin with my girl friend." Clearly, both of these persons believed to the point that they possessed intellectual assent, but their belief did not result in an obedient faith response.

It is not my desire just to present intellectual argument. You are not asked to believe merely in the sense of assenting to the fact that God exists, that Christ is God's Son, and that Scripture is inspired. Rather you are asked to respond to this study with an obedient, trusting faith. You should live a life of trusting work and worship in which God, His Spirit, and His Son Jesus Christ are your allies in every circumstance of life.

How Faith Develops

It is a mistake to equate *I believe* with the possession of a faith that pleases God. Obviously, anyone can say, "I believe." The process of faith development is much like the process that occurs when one learns to swim. A young boy who is first learning to swim may know intellectually that the buoyant effect of water will support him

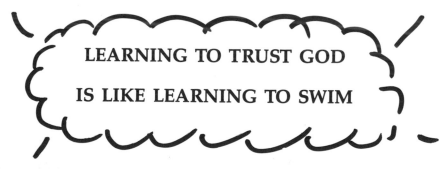

LEARNING TO TRUST GOD IS LIKE LEARNING TO SWIM

because he sees others floating. Although he may believe, he is nevertheless unwilling to commit himself to the water. Once confidence in the buoyant effect of water is developed by personal experience, he is then willing to trust and to move into deeper water.

6

Children, or even adults, may be taught that God exists, that Jesus is God's Son, and that the Bible is God's Word. They may even say, "I believe" yet be much like the person standing on the side of the pool, afraid to get into the water. Such persons have not yet processed faith intellectually and emotionally, and they are not willing to trust.

Parents are fulfilling a God-given responsibility when they teach their children to believe in God. However, unless faith is processed, it amounts to nothing more than an inherited faith. When crisis situations arise, it is not adequate because it is not personally owned. It frequently collapses, and we may say, "He lost his faith." The fact is that he had no personal faith in the first place. One cannot lose what one does not have.

Internalizing an inherited faith intellectually and emotionally may be a difficult, painful process. It is similar to the swimmer's moving into deep water, where the toes only occasionally touch the bottom of the pool. In fact, venturing into a trust relationship with God may be a frightening experience. This phase of faith development often coincides with the time when a young adult leaves home for work or college. At this vulnerable time, a person may encounter many different alternative faith systems. Unless his or her faith has already matured into a trust relationship with God, it is far better for that individual to continue to be nurtured in a supportive Christian environment.

The story of the blind man in John 9 is an excellent example of the faith process at work. As far as we know, the man whose blindness Jesus healed had never before encountered Christ. However, when he was told by Christ to go and wash away the clay spittle which had been placed on his eyes, he did as he was told. When he was first asked how he had regained his sight, he simply responded by relating the facts: "The man called Jesus made clay and anointed my eyes and said to me, 'Go to Siloam and wash;' so I went and washed and received my sight" (John 9:11). At this point, the healed beggar acknowledged Jesus as merely *a man*. Many men in Jerusalem were named "Jesus."

Since the healing occurred on the Sabbath, the Pharisees became annoyed because Jesus had practiced healing on the day of rest. The healed beggar's faith was put to its first test as the Pharisees called him to testify against Jesus, whom they accused of violating the Sabbath. The beggar's faith had had little time to be processed in his heart and mind. When he was asked by the Pharisees, "What do you say about him, since he has opened your eyes?" he answered, "He is a prophet" (John 9:17). Clearly, the healed beggar's estimation of Christ had changed from that of "a man named Jesus" to "a prophet." Acknowledging Jesus as a prophet, however, was far from acknowledging Him as the Son of God. For the healed beggar to admit that Jesus was the Son of God would have resulted in his being ejected from the synagogue and being removed from fellowship with the Pharisees (John 9:22).

Continuing the analogy of the developing of faith and learning to swim, the healed beggar was now in very deep water; only occasionally did his toes touch the bottom. Yet he had still not confessed Jesus Christ to be whom He claimed to be. As the interrogation became heated, the healed beggar knew that he must be true to the conviction of his heart. Under severe duress, he stated, "If this man were not from God, he could do nothing" (John 9:33). At that moment, he was expelled from synagogue fellowship.

To this point the healed beggar had not seen the form of the man who healed him, for he was blind when Jesus said, "Go wash." When Jesus heard that the man had been cast out of the synagogue, He found him and asked, "Do you believe?" The healed beggar then understood that the man who was speaking to him was his healer, and he responded by saying, " Lord, I believe" (John 9:38). He then worshipped Christ as the Son of God. At this point, we may say, the healed beggar was like the swimmer who casts himself confidently into very deep water and discovers that he can swim!

Walking By Faith

A study of both the Old and New Testaments reveals that God has always wanted man to walk by faith, yet man's preference has almost always been to walk by sight.

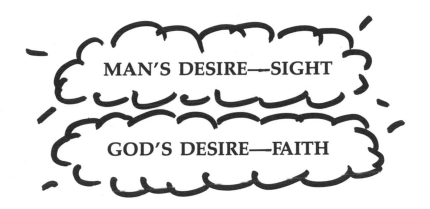

MAN'S DESIRE—SIGHT

GOD'S DESIRE—FAITH

The concept of faith, and especially God's desire for a trusting faith relationship with man, is repeatedly demonstrated in the Old Testament. The word *faith*, however, is used only two times in the Old Testament, and in one of those times, it is used in reference to Israel's *lack of faith* (Deuteronomy 32:20). The only other time the word is used is in Habakkuk 2:4 where the prophet wrote that "the righteous shall live by his faith." Here the word seems to be used in the same sense that it is used in the New Testament where the words *faith* and *believe* occur almost 500 times. Old Testament signs and New Testament miracles were sight demonstrations of God's existence and providence. Their purpose was to prepare Christians to live obediently in trusting faith by relying on God to keep His promises.

It is Abraham rather than Moses, David, or any other Old or New Testament character who is held up as the example of what a Christian's faith should be. Abraham's faith was not flawless. Nevertheless, it is his faith that we are taught to emulate. Why, then, is he our example of faith?

The incident in Abraham's life that established him as the father of the faithful was the offering of Isaac (Genesis 22, Romans 4). God promised Abraham that through his descendants all nations of the earth would be blessed (Genesis 12:1-3). When Abraham was ninety-nine years old and his wife Sarah was eighty-nine, they still had not been blessed with the child through whom the promise of God was to be fulfilled. Although Sarah laughed in disbelief when informed that she would have a child (Genesis 18:12), Abraham was "fully convinced that God was able to do what he had

9

promised" (Romans 4:21).

To be sure, many times over the next few years, Abraham must have looked upon young Isaac with great pride because he was the child through whom God's promise would be fulfilled. It is reasonable to suppose that Abraham experienced shock when he was told, "Take your son, your only son Isaac, whom you love, and go to the land of Moriah, and offer him there as a burnt offering upon one of the mountains of which I shall tell you" (Genesis 22:2). Abraham's faith did not fail as he moved with confidence and prepared to obey God.

After three days of travel, Abraham, two servants, and Isaac arrived at the foot of Mt. Moriah. Abraham revealed his confidence in God, believing that God would raise Isaac from the dead if necessary (Hebrews 11:19). He said to the servants, "Stay here, . . . I and the lad will go yonder and worship, and [we will] come again to you" (Genesis 22:5). This act of unwavering faith certified Abraham as "father of all the faithful" and typifies the kind of trust that God desires of all who believe in him.

In contrast to Abraham of the Old Testament, who is credited with walking by faith, Thomas of the New Testament, on one occasion, walked by sight (John 20). Probably most of us feel that we relate more to Thomas than to Abraham because the desire for sight or tangible experiences is a basic human weakness.

The rumor of the empty tomb of Jesus—after the crucifixion— finally reached Thomas. Perhaps we should be grateful that there was one disciple who was not easily convinced. When Thomas heard about the empty tomb, he stated, "Unless I see in his hands the print of the nails, and place my finger in the mark of the nails, and place my hand in his side, I will not believe" (John 20:25).

In all fairness to Thomas, we should be slow to criticize him for wanting to see the resurrected Christ. We must remember that Thomas, with his own eyes, had probably seen some graphic and impressionable sights: nails driven into the Savior's hands and feet, and the pierced side from which blood and water flowed. Thomas may also have heard with his own ears the sounds of death: cries of cursing and pleas for mercy from the executed thieves, gasps of dying men, and, finally, the words of the Lord, "Father, into thy hands I commit my spirit!" (Luke 23:46) Thomas may have wanted to see the nail prints because he had seen and heard the sounds of death.

In many respects, all of us today who believe are like Thomas. We did not walk the streets and plains of Judea with Christ; we did not see him put upon the cross; we did not gaze into the open tomb. Yet Christ pronounced a special blessing upon all of us who did not see these things but believe, worship, and serve Him: "Blessed are those who have not seen and yet believe" (John 20:29).

Conclusion

The Christian should offer no apology for the fact that he walks by faith instead of sight. Once he understands the meaning, scope, and significance of biblical faith, he will not want to apologize for having faith. Everyone walks by some kind of faith, but there is no faith among men, not even among today's scientists, that produces a greater degree of certainty than faith in Christ. Because of Christ, the Christian's walk in faith can be confident and assured. Faith is better than sight.

When my love to Christ grows weak,
When for deeper faith I seek,
Then in tho't I go to thee,
Garden of Gethsemane.
                    J. R. Wreford

2

How Should I Respond To Doubt?

Walking by faith in the midst of confidence and certainty sounds inviting. However, some Christians do not feel confident and certain in their faith in every circumstance. Life is often unfair, and, at those times, it is difficult to maintain a faith that does not waver.

Today there is a widespread teaching that is potentially very damaging to faith. Well-meaning but misguided persons teach a message which is almost certain to destroy the very faith it espouses. That message says, "If you will embrace Christian faith, you will be a *success* in life, and all of your troubles will be over." Neither Christ nor any of His apostles made such a promise.

No faith can guarantee *success* in life or freedom from life's crises and calamities. Failure, disaster, disease, and death are a part of the common lot of man regardless of the faith by which he chooses to live. Although Christianity does not guarantee freedom from life's crises, it is the best faith alternative by which one can live in the midst of crisis. Christianity, likewise, does not guarantee that the Christian will be free of doubt and uncertainty. However, Christianity does offer the best possible solution to the doubt and uncertainty experienced by everyone at one time or another.

ATHEISTS HAVE DOUBTS TOO

The atheist says, "There is no God." Do you not suppose there are occasions when even the world's most notable atheist on a clear, dark night looks into the Milky Way constellation and wonders, "What if there really is a God who will hold me accountable"? Do you not suppose that even the most avowed materialist ponders, "Can I possibly be wrong? What if mind *did* precede matter"? The Christian has no monopoly on doubt—just as the Christian has no monopoly on faith.

The Relationship Between Faith and Doubt

Many people believe that faith and doubt are opposites. It is important to understand, however, that faith and doubt are not on opposing ends of a belief continuum as the following biblical example illustrates.

FAITH AND DOUBT ARE NOT OPPOSITES

A concerned father brought his son to Jesus. The boy was sporadically cast into convulsions, during which he would roll on the ground, foam at the mouth, or fall into fire or pools of water (Mark 9:14-29). The father, desiring to have Jesus heal his son, said, "If you can do anything, have pity on us and help us." Jesus replied, "If you can! All things are possible to him who believes." Immediately, the father cried out and said, "I believe; help my unbelief."

We can perhaps better understand this story if we look through the eyes of a loving father who had frequently seen his boy convulsing upon the ground or falling into fire. Surely the father of the boy would have given anything in his possession if his son could have been relieved of the torture his body experienced on those awful occasions.

It is apparent that when the afflicted boy's father said to Jesus, "I believe; help my unbelief," he actually meant something other than what he said. Belief and unbelief are complete opposites. The mind cannot simultaneously entertain belief and unbelief. What the father meant was, "I believe; help me in my doubt," or "I believe, but help me in those areas where I have difficulty believing." The boy's father clearly wanted to believe that Jesus had the power to heal his son, and he wanted to yield to the authority of Jesus' power. Yet he had difficulty believing. His desire was for Christ to remove whatever was hindering his belief. Most of us have, at one time or another, shared the same frustration.

Although a person may claim that he has never entertained doubt, it is likely that the person who has never doubted has developed very little faith. Our intention is not to encourage doubt, but, just as iron sharpens iron, doubt sharpens faith if it receives the proper response. A mind that uses the intellect as a part of the faith process will experience doubt.

Many biblical characters doubted. Yet you will not find an example of anyone in the Bible who encouraged another to doubt the fundamental teachings of Jewish or Christian faith and did so with God's blessings. Nevertheless, a study of the Scriptures also shows that experiencing doubt is an essential part of the faith process. People of faith experience doubt for many reasons.

Reasons for Doubt

In Chapter 1 we learned that faith development is a process; that is, obedient, trusting faith does not come suddenly. Biblical faith initially comes by hearing (Romans 10:17). That one hears and intellectually agrees that God exists and that Jesus is Divine does not mean he has obedient, trusting faith. Almost everyone initially believes by hearing spiritual truth from a significant adult—such as a parent, friend, or teacher. At this stage, he has a faith that is merely inherited. However, as he grows in faith he progresses from having an inherited faith to having a faith that he owns.

HOW FAITH DEVELOPS

FAITH	FAITH	FAITH
INHERITED	TESTED	OWNED

In order for faith to progress from the inherited stage to the stage in which it is personally owned, faith must be *tested*. Faith is tested by life's daily natural circumstances. Here we see the reason why Christians should "count it all joy. . .when they meet various trials" (James 1:2): *it is through experience that faith matures and becomes personally owned.*

Herein is also the first reason why some Christians doubt. A person with an inherited faith will not respond to a faith crisis in the same way as a person whose faith has already been tested and has matured. The Christian life is a process of the gradual transformation of a person who initially believes into one who possesses the mind of Christ. One is naturally far more susceptible to doubt early in the transformation process. This fact recommends that mature Christians should be benevolent toward younger Christians who frequently experience doubt.

A second reason why some doubt is that they may not be willing to pay the price of believing. Believing in Christ and His teachings may require the adoption of a life-style completely opposite to that to which one has become accustomed. The price of believing is obedience. According to John, one who does not obey does not believe (John 3:36, *RSV*). Many people avoid faith in God because they are not willing to obey.

One implication of the existence of God that many find unacceptable is moral responsibility. If God has created man in His image, man is morally responsible, and moral responsibility is inconsistent with a life-style oriented toward hedonistic pleasures. The only way to live a Playboy or Playgirl life-style is to doubt or

16

to discard Christian faith altogether.

A third reason why people doubt is that they dare to ask hard questions—questions which nurture doubt. This is not to say that hard questions should be avoided. Since God created man's intelligence, He expects man to ask difficult questions. Paul says, "Test everything; hold fast what is good" (1 Thessalonians 5:21). It is not an insult to God to ask why there is so much evil in the world. It is reasonable to expect an intelligent individual to ask, "Why would a benevolent God allow 2,000 birth defects to result in congenital disorders?" "Why would He allow the atrocities of a Hitler or Stalin?" "Why would a lovely, young Christian girl be killed in an automobile accident by a drunken driver?" These are indeed difficult questions, but there is no shame in verbalizing them. In fact, there is honor in seeking meaningful answers. In the process that leads to answers, the best minds of every generation have, on occasion, experienced doubt. It is indeed better to have asked and experienced doubt than never to have asked at all, for in the process of asking and searching, answers come, and faith matures.

A fourth reason for doubting is that the inquiring mind is always discovering new evidence—evidence which may challenge faith. One's response to new evidence may be to avoid new learning situations altogether and simply avoid exposure to information which may cause doubt. In college, one may avoid a career in psychology because some behavioral theory is based in humanism. One may avoid a career in the sciences because of the threat of chemical and biological evolution. To be sure, any Christian who pursues a career in these—and many other fields of study—is going to experience doubt. However, if he correctly responds to doubt as it arises, he will overcome his doubt, and faith will be enriched and matured. This approach is preferred over avoiding difficult fields of study such as psychology and the natural sciences.

A fundamental belief of Christian faith is that all truth has its origin in God. When questions that threaten faith arise in any field of study, the Christian should not be afraid to search for answers. As a student on a state college campus, I was told that Jesus Christ is no different from Confucius, Buddha, or any other great spiritual leader. My initial reaction was one of fear and dread. I was fearful that my informant was right, and I dreaded discovering the truth of the matter.

17

Finally, I went to the bookstore where I purchased a copy of the sayings of Confucius, and to the library where I checked out and read the best literature I could find on living world religions. I discovered that Confucius is not a religious leader and Confucianism is only an ethical system with no concept of sin or redemption. However, it does have merit for the value of its ethical teachings. My study led me to the conclusion that Christ has no peer among world religious leaders, living or dead, and that Christianity has no equal among world religions, present or past.

We must not be afraid to compare Christ or Christianity with the best that human philosophy has to offer. C. S. Lewis has correctly observed that Christ is either lunatic or Lord.[1] Christ does not deserve our allegiance if He is not everything He claims to be. In the pages to follow, we will present evidence that Christ is precisely who He claims to be—the Son of God.

For many years science and mathematics majors at Harding University who are enrolled in a course designed to reinforce faith have been asked, "What bothers your faith most?" One of the responses most frequently given, and our fifth reason why Christians doubt, is "the way I see some Christians treating other Christians." One's initial reaction may be that this is a weak response and that these students have not experienced severe tests of their faith. However, the visible evidence that God exists and that Jesus Christ is His son is seen in the way Christ's disciples treat one another (John 17:21).

The church is the visible body of Christ on earth today. Fragmenting His body into parts which do not communicate with or fellowship with one another is a horrid evil. The fact that this has already occurred is, for many, the greatest deterrent to the development of faith. Division within the body of Christ is *not* Christ's desire. Fragmentation is the result of man's evil actions, not the work of God's Holy Spirit. The solution to overcoming this threat to faith is for the Christian who truly wishes to be Christ's disciple to look beyond divisive human tendencies to Christ, who desires that we love one another.

Sixth, some people doubt or even discard the Christian alternative because they misunderstand Christian doctrine. Bertrand Russell was a world-renowned mathematical logician. Early in his career he delivered a series of lectures which were later published under

18

the title *Why I Am Not A Christian*.[2] It is apparent from reading the lectures that he had a poor concept of Christianity, and, that, partly for that reason, he rejected it. One reason why Russell was critical of Christianity was that he thought crimes done in the name of Christianity were sanctioned by the Bible. However, neither Christianity nor God was in any way responsible for such atrocities as the Spanish Inquisition or so-called "holy wars" fought in the name of Christianity.

Examples of Doubt

A common characteristic of all the great examples of the faithful recorded in Hebrews 11 is that they all doubted. Abraham is our example of one who trusted God to keep His promises. Yet Abraham experienced doubt. God called Abraham when he lived in the land of Ur in Mesopotamia (Acts 7:2) and instructed him to go to the land of Canaan (Genesis 11:31). However, he settled in Haran, and God had to call him a second time (Genesis 12:1). After eventually settling in Canaan, Abraham migrated to Egypt because there was a famine in Canaan. In Egypt, Abraham, for fear of his own life, passed off Sarah, his wife, to Pharaoh as his sister (Genesis 12:12ff). Sarah was actually a half-sister to Abraham, but his intended deception led God to intervene and bring plagues upon the house of Pharaoh. Later, in the land of the Negeb, he practiced the same deception (Genesis 20:2).

Again, God renewed the promise of the land of Canaan to Abraham. His response to God was to ask, "How am I to *know* that I shall possess it?" (Genesis 15:8). Abraham, in asking for a sign, was not walking by faith. He was walking by sight. Nevertheless, God accommodated him in his doubt. Eventually, he overcame his doubt and learned that he could, without reservation, trust in God, who keeps His promises.

Moses was the great Old Testament deliverer of the people of God. God, through Moses, directed the people of Israel from Egyptian slavery to the promised land of Canaan. We would find it difficult to produce an example of one who was more intimately drawn into the presence of God than was Moses. Nevertheless, the story of Moses' life is one of great faith occasionally in tension with doubt by the burning bush at the time of Moses' call (Exodus 3). Although Moses talked directly with God, he still required two signs and the assurance of Aaron's support as spokesman before he consented to accept God's call.

Leading more than a million people across the Red Sea into the wilderness, Moses performed miracle after miracle which constantly reminded him of the direct presence of God. At Marah bitter waters were sweetened. At Elim the Israelites were providentially refreshed by twelve springs of water and seventy palms. In the Wilderness of Sin manna from Heaven fed the people. At Rephidim Moses, as spokesman for God, commanded and water gushed forth from a rock. At Sinai Moses received the ten commandments directly from God.

Later, when God told Moses to speak to a rock to produce water, Moses decided to do it his way and struck the rock instead. For his disobedience, Moses gave up his right to enter the Land of Canaan. Moses is a great example of trusting, obedient faith. Yet he knew the disappointment of wavering faith.

Before being critical of others for doubting, we should imagine how we would have responded had we been in their places. For example, John the Baptist had been imprisoned by Herod for condemning the king's sins. There probably has never been a more confident and stern preacher than John. At Christ's baptism, John acknowledged Jesus as Messiah. Yet in prison, John doubted.

The conditions of John's imprisonment were far from the conditions found in most modern prisons. It is likely that John's cell was underground and poorly lighted, if lighted at all. The prison was probably cold, damp, and insect-infested. A new day would possibly bring the palace guards to get a prisoner for execution. Under such conditions, John had second thoughts and sent word by his disciples, asking Christ, "Are you he who is to come, or shall we look for another?" (Matthew 11:2). In this statement we see doubt, but we do not see despair. We see a mixture of doubt and confidence.

Is It a Sin to Doubt?

It is not our intention here to encourage doubt or to portray it in a favorable light. However, doubt is an inevitable part of the process by which trusting, obedient faith develops. God was not pleased when Abraham lied, Sarah laughed, or Moses argued. Likewise, God is not pleased when we doubt His existence or His promises to us. Surely, Elijah must have expressed God's disappointment in a doubting Israel when he cried out on Mount Carmel, "How long will you go limping with two different opinions?" (1 Kings 18:21). Christ probably looks upon us in our doubt with the same disappointment as He did Peter when He asked, "O man of little faith, why did you doubt"? (Matthew 14:31).

As Christian fathers and mothers, we are disappointed when our children doubt our judgment or question our wisdom. God, as our Father, is surely disappointed when we doubt His word or His existence. Nevertheless, the evidence from Scripture is that it is not so much the doubt that determines sin as it is the response to doubt. One does not necessarily cease to believe when he doubts, but he does not believe with equal intensity or confidence.

Romans 14:23 has been understood to mean that all doubt is sin: "Whatsoever is not of faith is sin" (*KJV*). This verse is misused and abused if taken as proof that all doubt is necessarily sinful. The context in which Paul writes relates to the eating of meat that had been offered to idols. Although not included in the above translation, the word "action" is implied. In other words, the intended message is "Whatsoever action (eating of meat offered to idols) that is not done in faith is sinful." The conclusion, then, is that doubt itself may not be sinful, but acting upon one's doubt is sinful. *It is one's response to doubt that determines whether he sins.*

How Should One Respond to Doubt?

One cannot avoid all circumstances in life that seem to be fertile soil for doubt, apprehension, and uncertainty. We have some, but often little, control over circumstances. Nevertheless, there are some helpful things one can do when doubt arises. First, make it a point to associate with those who will help you think positively in circumstances that lead to doubt. Since faith comes from what is heard (Romans 10:17), be diligent in attending devotionals, Bible classes, and worship, where God's word is taught and where the warmth of Christian fellowship is experienced and nurtured.

21

Second, when you are inclined to doubt, pray—even if you do not feel like praying. The prophet Jeremiah (12:1) and Asaph, who apparently wrote Psalm 73, both doubted when they saw the prosperity of the wicked. However, both found refuge in Jehovah and, in the words of the Psalmist, "It seemed to me a wearisome task, until I went into the sanctuary of God" (Psalm 73:16, 17). In times of doubt and apprehension it may seem that God is far, far away. However, that is when He draws nearest to His sons and daughters to provide the special strength they need.

Third, when doubt comes, remember that Christian faith is not inferior to other faith alternatives. It is not true that the Christian relies on faith while others rely on knowledge. *Everyone* relies on faith. It is not a question of whether we will walk by faith, but rather, "By which faith will we *choose* to walk?" Human philosophy, which is not based in God, leads to despair. But Christians are not left to despair. Christ gives us an understanding of our origin and purpose. He gives meaning to existence as He interprets reality for us.

Fourth, when you are inclined to doubt, remember that crises and tribulations in life are inevitable. It is through meeting affliction *with God* that the Christian life takes on full significance. Paul, at Lystra, after having been stoned and left for dead, revived and continued "strengthening the souls of the disciples, exhorting them to continue in the faith, and saying that through many tribulations we must enter the kingdom of God" (Acts 14:22).

In reason's ear they all rejoice,
And utter forth a glorious voice,
Forever singing as they shine,
The hand that made us is Divine.
                    Joseph Addison

3

Does Faith in God Make Sense?

Does God exist? No question has more fundamental or far-reaching significance than the question of God's existence. The answer to the question determines man's concept of himself and his duty toward his fellow man. If God exists, then you, I, and every other intelligent person who has ever lived or ever will live are morally responsible beings. If God does not exist, no argument remains for moral responsibility.

GOD'S EXISTENCE DOES NOT DEPEND ON WHAT ANYONE THINKS ABOUT GOD

What one desires, thinks, or feels about God's existence has no bearing on whether God exists. God either exists, or He does not exist. Ten thousand theologians or atheists shouting from now until eternity will not alter what is true about God. But can we know whether God exists? Can we possess certainty beyond reasonable doubt that God exists or that He does not exist? Or must we rely only on a blind leap of unsubstantiated faith? God cannot be seen through a microscope or a telescope; He cannot be measured or tested by laboratory instruments. Is a belief in God comparable to believing in superstitions?

The purpose of the next two chapters is to demonstrate that the question of God's existence does not belong in the category of superstition. Furthermore, the fact that God cannot be measured or tested by laboratory instruments does not negate His existence. We do not dismiss the existence of human emotions and declare them to be superstition because they cannot be empirically tested. Scientists do not dismiss the existence of electrons because they cannot be individually seen; neither should we dismiss God because He cannot be captured in a test tube.

There are three avenues by which evidence on the question of God's existence is open to us—the testimonies of reason, nature, and biblical revelation. Inasmuch as we will later present evidence on the trustworthiness of biblical revelation, the next two chapters will concentrate on evidence for the existence of God which comes from human reason and nature.

Can God's Existence Be Proved?

Even among Christian believers, emotions may be deeply aroused in response to the question, "Can God's existence be proved?" Some feel threatened by any reliance at all on faith and demand that God's existence be proved to the exclusion of faith. Others claim that God's existence cannot be proved at all. The problem may be resolved, in part, by inspecting a good dictionary for the meanings of the words *faith* and *prove*. Doing so will demonstrate that both words can be used in a variety of ways. I hope it is clear that I have been convinced by heritage, experience, evidence, and persuasion that God does exist. Therefore, in this sense, *God's existence has been proved to me*. It would, therefore, be untruthful for me to say that God's existence cannot be proved in at least one sense of the word.

Sometimes the word *prove* is used to mean that "biblical faith is excluded." I freely acknowledge that God's existence cannot be proved in that sense of the word. It is clear from Scripture that God calls man on the basis of faith which is supported by evidence and not on proof or demonstration which excludes faith (Genesis 1:1; Hebrews 11:1,3,6). I recall having a roommate in college who said, "If God wants me to believe in Him, let Him show Himself to me." We cannot expect to respond to God on that kind of evidence.

The authors of the Bible do not attempt to systematically prove God. Rather they take the position that God's existence is self-evident and that this conclusion is more reasonable than any other conclusion. All that Scripture says about God is in harmony with the declaration of Genesis 1:1: "In the beginning God." Throughout the Old Testament, God challenged false gods and prophets and decried any person or nation who created an idol and worshiped it as God. In Romans 1:19 and 20 Paul states that God's existence is self-evident:

> For what can be known about God is plain to them, because God has shown it to them. Ever since the creation of the world his invisible nature, namely, his eternal power and deity, has been clearly perceived in the things that have been made. So they are without excuse.

Consistent with this declaration, Paul also acknowledges God's existence as self-evident in the Athenian sermon (Acts 17). Likewise, I do not philosophize, theorize, or speculate about God. I am confident that God exists and that "in him we live and move and have our being" (Acts 17:28). *By faith I acknowledge God as the most fundamental, self-evident Truth in reality.*

Many, however, are not convinced of God's existence. *Atheists* believe that God does not exist. *Agnostics* believe that God may exist but that it is impossible to know for sure whether He exists. *Skeptics* are very much like agnostics in that they habitually doubt, question, or ridicule the beliefs of others. *Deists* believe that if God exists, He stands apart from reality. To the deists, God's role ceased after He created natural law; the universe, therefore, exhibits the appearance of a clock which God initially wound up but which now runs completely independent of His intervention. *Pantheists* believe that everything in nature is God and that God is everything in nature. According to their view, God exists in the rocks, rivers, mountains, insects, and every other aspect of nature. God is, therefore, not a personality, but all of nature, including natural law, is a manifestation of God.

Is It a Toss-up?

Some people think that not believing in God is as reasonable as believing in God. In other words, one might as well toss a coin to determine whether to have faith in God. That is not true. When all the evidence is in and carefully weighed, belief in God provides a far more satisfactory faith by which to live than belief in the nonexistence of God.

You are reminded of our conclusion that everyone is going to have faith in something. The choice is yours. Do you want to live by faith in the existence of God and the implications of that faith, or do you want to live by faith in the nonexistence of God and the implications of that faith? God does not expect you to make an emotional response to these questions; He expects you to make a rational, intellectual response. On the pages that follow, you are given a basis on which to make a careful, intellectual response to God.

Moral Freedom To Choose

The fact that you possess the moral freedom to choose between believing in God or not believing in God is itself evidence that God exists. If God does not exist, thoughts are nothing more than atoms and molecules in motion. In fact, the human body and brain consist essentially of only about twelve elements such as carbon, hydrogen, oxygen, nitrogen, and sulfur. No physical or biological law gives us a basis for assuming that any assemblage of the elements of the human body should produce matter which has the ability to think, much less to make choices. If perchance an accidental assemblage of chemical elements should be able to think, you would not expect it to have thoughts of anything beyond atoms and molecules. You would not expect it to have thoughts of moral responsibility and God.

I once heard a biochemist speak who was on tour for the American Chemical Society. While speaking on the subject of the chemical basis of thought, he stated that all mental processes are but accidental collisions of atoms and molecules. When he was asked, "How then do you account for the ability of a person to make moral decisions?" he responded, "There is no human will; there can be no moral decision." He was a materialist; that is, one who believes that matter is all there is.

This biochemist could not know that man does not have a will and that man cannot make moral choices; his faith in the nonexistence of God demanded that he deny the existence of the human will. He went on to conclude that right and wrong do not exist. He said that we should tear down all prisons and jails and place prisoners in hospitals, for they are not "bad" but sick. Belief in the nonexistence of God leaves no basis for moral decision, for it concludes that right and wrong are nothing more than social conveniences.

It is of interest that this biochemist and his family were refugees from Communist East Germany and had fled to the West to avoid Communist persecution. According to his belief, the Communists were just as "right" in practicing social injustice and persecution as he and his family were "right" in fleeing. However, man is not merely a robot controlled by the accidental arrangement of atoms and molecules. He is not a little higher than a brute beast; he is a little lower than the angels, created in the image of God and endowed with the responsibility of moral decision.

You would rightfully be insulted if you were told that you were incapable of making decisions. Yet that is precisely what many who deny existence of God would have you believe. A psychology professor entered the classroom in which I once sat and stated, "You are not here because you chose to come to this class. Rather, you are here because of prior events which have occurred in your life which *determined* that you would be here at this very moment."

Little did the college freshmen realize that the professor was speaking from the background of his faith in materialistic determinism, which is atheistic. Determinism claims that all present events, including choices, are the result of previous events. Hence, if determinism is true, human will and choices are ruled out.

The supposition that reality is deterministic has had a major influence on human philosophy. Atheistic materialism is deterministic, for it does not allow for the existence of the human will or for choices of any kind. There was a time when scientists and philosophers believed that once we knew enough about molecular processes, we would be able to predict all future human conduct. Today, scientists and philosophers generally recognize the futility of such a claim.

Humanity's Desire to Worship

One who does not believe in the existence of God faces a formidable question: "If God does not exist, why has man throughout the ages desired to worship some concept of deity?" Upon arriving at Athens (Acts 17), the Apostle Paul observed that the Athenians worshiped many gods. Lest they overlooked one of the gods, they had erected a sign "to an unknown god." Paul did not criticize them for having concluded that Deity exists; rather he proceeded to declare to them the nature of God whom they ignorantly worshiped.

To be sure, man has worshiped deities in a wide variety of ways, but man has always worshiped. Egyptian Pharaohs were buried with boats to aid them on their journeys into the spirit land; North American Indians anticipated a happy hunting ground; South American Indians worshiped the sun god. No ancient or modern civilization has existed that has not, in some way, expressed itself in worship. This cannot be passed off as a common superstition. There *must* be a rational explanation for man's common desire to reach beyond himself in worship. That explanation is God.

The Whole Is More Than the Sum of Its Parts

A fundamental assumption in the physical and biological world is that the whole is equal to, but never more than, the sum of its parts. For example, the Law of Conservation of Matter and Energy states that the energy content of the universe is fixed, that is, constant. Stated another way, this law tells us that matter is neither being created nor destroyed. However, it is impossible to understand our world by assuming that it consists only of atoms and molecules. In many cases, the whole is clearly more than the sum of its parts.

Although a rock or a medical prescription may safely be thought equal to the sum of its parts, many a person would argue that the rule does not apply to his favorite pet. Certainly the rule does not apply to man. Man has a spirit and personality not found in atoms and molecules.

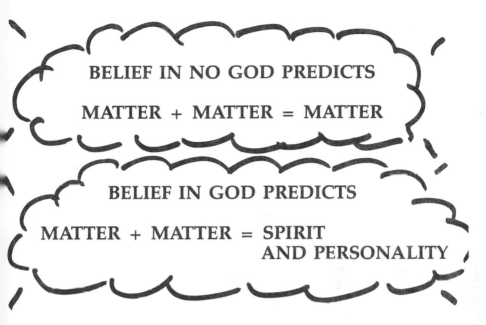

BELIEF IN NO GOD PREDICTS

MATTER + MATTER = MATTER

BELIEF IN GOD PREDICTS

MATTER + MATTER = SPIRIT
AND PERSONALITY

If man consists solely of nonpersonal atoms and molecules, one would expect him to have the personality of a robot, but one would not expect him to have human personality as we know it. Human personality stems from the fact that man has a spirit because he has been created by God in the image of God.

Physical Law Implies a Lawgiver

When we encounter a highway sign that reads, "Speed Zone Ahead," we recognize the universally accepted truth that law is established only by authority. The road sign is there because someone had the authority to place it there. Likewise, the existence of law in the natural realm implies an authoritative Law-Giver who created law in nature. For example, the universe is governed by physical laws such as the law of gravity, the laws of motion, and the laws which govern space and time.

Laws of chemistry govern the chemical combination of the elements, the rates of chemical reactions, and chemical thermodynamics. These physical laws can be studied, experimentally evaluated, and mathematically formulated—but they cannot be violated. The logical conclusion is that these laws exist because a Law-Giver created the physical universe.

All matter in the universe consists of units called atoms. Atomic structure and bonding between atoms is not haphazard; it is carefully governed by exact laws of chemical bonding. These natural laws suggest the existence of an infinitely wise Law-Giver.

Atoms combine by laws which govern chemical reactions to form molecules. Molecules further combine to form matter. Beautiful, highly ordered crystals are formed when molecules are allowed to combine under the right conditions. Fundamental physical laws govern the tendency of molecules to become ordered in such crystal arrangements.

Natural physical law has operated over time to produce the Grand Canyon, Yosemite Valley, and other strikingly beautiful geological earth features. Many scientific theories prevail to explain how the earth's surface is being shaped. However, we may be confident that all of the processes involved operate by law—law which was created and is sustained by the Law-Giver, God. Because of reliable natural physical laws, man has been able to put satellites in orbit around the earth, walk on the moon, and send exploratory satellites through our solar system and beyond.

Biological Law Implies a Law-Giver

Biological law governs living things just as physical law governs nonliving things. However, living things are far more complex than nonliving things. For this reason, it is impossible to reduce life to mathematically formulated law. The complexity of life leads us to conclude that biological processes are governed by biological law.

Unparalleled beauty, order, and design are apparent in living things leading us to the conclusion that underlying life principles are not haphazard. We think of orderly phenomena such as cell division; transference of genetic information; asexual and sexual reproduction; plant pollination; colonization of insects; animal instinct; and symmetry in the plant and animal kingdoms. Again, there appear to be only two alternatives: we can attribute biological law and order to God as Law-Giver, or we can attribute it to chance and random processes alone.

30

Animal Migration

Animal instinct is particularly intriguing. For example, freshwater American and European eels grow to sexual maturity for five to fifteen years thousands of miles apart on two different continents. Then, upon nature's signal, they leave the fresh waters of both continents and migrate to one of the deepest and saltiest regions of the oceans in the Sargasso Sea of the South Atlantic near Bermuda.

In the Sargasso Sea the mature eels spawn and then die leaving only tiny larval eels. The larval eels grow to a few inches in length. Then, again at nature's signal and without the direction of their parents, the larval eels begin a seemingly impossible journey—the journey back home to the fresh water streams of America and Europe.

It takes the American eels fifteen months to find their way back home through the ocean currents, then up the rivers to the streams where they grow to maturity. It takes the European eels three years to find their way back home because the journey is much longer. The larval eels make this entire journey without the assistance of their parents who died in the Sargasso Sea.

This behavior of the American and European eels is indeed perplexing to biologists and is one of nature's most phenomenal wonders. On the action of the eels, Harvard University biology professor and winner of the Nobel Prize, George Wald, recently stated, "...the action of the eels—points unmistakably to the idea of a pervasive mind intertwined and inseparable from the material universe"[1]. Wald also acknowledged that "this conclusion about mind embarrasses biologists" [2] However, we should observe that his conclusion only embarrasses *some* biologists; it does not embarrass a biologist who believes in the existence of God.

Can Scientists Create Life?

Some believe that if scientists ever succeed in synthesizing life in the laboratory, the need for God will be eliminated. In fact, I was in graduate school with a very intelligent young man who believed in God. However, one day he stated, "If scientists ever succeed in

31

creating life, I will no longer believe in God." This conclusion is a great mistake. First, we do not suppose that God exists just so we can explain things science cannot. Secondly, if life is totally synthesized in the laboratory, it will be intelligence that accomplishes the synthesis. In fact, the total synthesis of life by scientists, if it occurs, will further demonstrate the need for an Original Intelligence, God.

Cause and Effect

A law fundamental to the understanding of the physical universe is the Law of Cause and Effect. This concept is based on the assumption that every effect must have an adequate cause. This means that something never comes from nothing and that every material thing must have a reason for being. The Christian believes that God is the universal First Cause, or the Prime Mover of the universe. He also believes that God is eternal. The materialist, on the other hand, believes that matter is eternal. Presently, the best theory that materialists have for the origin of the universe is that it came into existence perhaps twenty billion years ago from an unknown source of concentrated energy no larger than the head of a pin.

The universe requires a creator just as every house that is built requires an architect and builder. The Hebrew writer states this thought well, "For every house is built by some one, but the builder of all things is God" (Hebrews 3:4). Cosmologists now virtually agree that the universe has not existed forever; there must have been a beginning, currently called the Big Bang. The most recent theories advanced by astrophysicists hold that the universe resulted from an explosion of pure, pent-up, exquisitely hot, primordial energy. Yet physical theory cannot account for the origin of the energy or the conditions which existed before or resulted in the Big Bang.

Our solar system consists of nine planets, an asteroid belt, and an average-sized star, the sun. In comparison, if the sun were the size of a basketball and were placed on the goal line of a football field, our earth would be the size of a BB shot on the nearest thirty-yard line. There are stars in our galaxy 100 times larger than our sun, and other stars one hundredth the size of our sun.

Our galaxy is spiral-shaped and contains an estimated 100 billion (100,000,000,000) suns. However, astronomers tell us there may be an additional 200 billion galaxies—each with as many stars as our galaxy contains. At the speed of light, it would take 100,000 years to traverse our galaxy. It would take another 150,000 years to reach our nearest neighboring galaxy, the Magellanic Clouds, which can barely be seen with the naked eye from the southern hemisphere.

We understand that something as relatively simple as a watch could not just happen into existence, even given indefinite time. The same logic must apply to the origin of our solar system or universe. For a watch or the universe to exist, there must have been a designer, creator, and organizer. Footprints in the sand tell us that someone has passed this way before. It is likewise reasonable to suppose that the existence of the universe, as well as its apparent order and design, also tells us that God exists. In fact, everything that we see on the broad spectrum of nature, from the microscopic world to the cosmic world, teaches us to trust the Creator whom we have not seen.

Conclusion

All streams flow from their source to the sea. The flow of a stream never, without assistance, rises above its source. Likewise, no known physical or biological law suggests that the properties of instinct, mind, personality, intelligence, will, morality, or law would arise entirely by accident due to a natural flow of matter without the assistance of a Divine Being. Faith in God makes sense.

The unwearied sun from day to day
does his Creator's power display,
And publishes to every land
the work of an almighty hand.
                    Joseph Addison

4

What Does Nature Tell Us About God?

The word *teleology* comes from the Greek root word *telos,* meaning "end, purpose." Teleology is, therefore, a study of final, or ultimate, causes and suggests that design and purpose are evident in nature.

Christian parents typically use teleological language when they explain natural events to their children. For example, a child may ask, "How does a seed turn into a plant?" Most Christian parents have explained seed germination to their children by saying, "God causes the seed to produce a plant so that it will make more seeds and we can have food." This is a teleological explanation because it answers the question of seed germination by reference to God, an ultimate cause, and proposes there is purpose in seed germination.

It should be apparent that teleological explanations are not scientific explanations. They are not scientific because science, a purely human enterprise, cannot address final or ultimate causes. Scientific explanations are necessarily limited to *descriptions* of natural events. Most persons who deny God discount teleological explanations altogether and claim that all natural processes are caused by chance alone. Scientists who believe in God—and there are many—do not hesitate to acknowledge God as the grand Designer of the universe. Apparent design and purpose in reality imply a Designer or Purposer. This is the basis for the teleological explanation for God's existence.

35

The Trap of the God of the Gaps

Teleological explanations are not without their problems for Christians. Let us return to the example of the child asking about seed germination. After the child is a few years older and has perhaps studied biology in high school, he may again ask, "How does a seed germinate to produce a new plant?" This time the answer he receives may be quite different from the answer he received earlier. The explanation now may be that germination occurs when the moisture content of the seed reaches 70 to 80 percent and the temperature of the soil is between 37⁰C and 45⁰C. These conditions are adequate to activate the enzymes necessary for DNA replication and protein synthesis. This would not be a teleological explanation because it has no reference to a final cause, God, or to design and purpose.

An alert student may take notice of the fact that at one stage God and purpose are used to explain seed germination. Later, however, natural process with no reference to God is used to explain how a seed produces a new plant. Some people conclude that scientific knowledge effectively squeezes God out and that, with the rapid advance of scientific knowledge in each generation, soon there will be no need for God at all. However, it is dangerous and inappropriate to use God to explain gaps in scientific knowledge. The Christian's God is not a God of gaps in knowledge; He is the God who stands behind all the truth of the universe, scientific and otherwise.

Even taking into consideration advances in scientific knowledge, a thoughtful person would find teleological explanation for God's existence stronger today than ever. Scientists have not explained away God by discovering mechanisms and processes. Rather, modern scientific discovery has served to highlight our need for God by uncovering, at deeper levels of understanding, the remarkable phenomena at work in nature. For example, in the seed illustration cited, the process of DNA replication and enzyme activation is no less than remarkable.

Scientific investigation is like peeling an infinite onion. Once natural phenomena are understood at one level, another level remains at which the same phenomena can be studied. With each successive explanation, scientists expose more evidence that reveals an underlying design, order, and purpose to reality. Certainly world scientists are not busy intentionally proving the existence of the Christian's God. However, God is the best of all possible faith alternatives for explaining the apparent architectural design in the universe.

Only three alternatives seem to exist as one attempts to account for apparent design and purpose in reality: (a) reality is a figment of our (or some super being's) imagination; (b) reality is attributable to chance and randomness; and (c) a God exists who is responsible for the evident design and purpose in the universe.

The suggestion that reality is not real begs the entire question of existence. It is impossible to prove to a person that both you and he are but figments of the imagination of some super being. Although some philosophical systems take the position that "realities are not true," we believe this is a nonsensical approach to reality. Any proposed solution to the problem of existence which denies existence cannot be taken very seriously.

Two alternatives remain: the universe and the intelligence that inhabits it are either the products of chance and randomness, or they are the products of an intelligent Designer. We offer the following specific examples of evidence in support of the position that God is the Designer and Purposer of the universe.

Intelligence: A Masterpiece of Design

Our universe is indeed a collection of intriguing phenomena. There are neutron stars in which matter the size of a pea weighs more than 130,000,000 tons. Far denser, however, are black holes which are so dense that any energy or object which moves close to them is sucked in, devoured, and lost forever. Black holes emit no energy because gravitation is so strong within them that energy cannot escape. Evidence indicates that they exist, but they must forever be observed indirectly. Intriguing within our grand universe are island universes or galaxies. Within galaxies, stars are described as dwarfs, giants, and super giants. Yet all of these phenomenal features are much less intriguing than human intelligence. That the universe exists is not so remarkable—more so is that you or I can perceive the universe.

It is an understatement to say that the human brain, by its design, is an architectural masterpiece which only Deity could contrive. No one would dare say that a computer is not designed. Yet modern computer research focuses on how the brain functions to enable computer-design engineers to create more powerful, effective machines. If the age of artificial computer intelligence arrives, it will most likely do so because we have learned more about how the human brain works.

A single human adult brain weighs about three pounds and contains 100 billion (a billion is 1,000 million) nerve cells called neurons and 900 billion (nine times the number of stars in our galaxy) neuroglia. Neuroglia are specialized connecting and supporting cells of the brain and spinal cord. Yet the myriad of cells and component parts of the brain are so designed and ordered, within a volume smaller than a shoe box, that the human brain thinks, creates, contemplates, loves, hates, senses, and worships.

The central nervous system in general, and the human brain in particular, possibly constitute the strongest teleological argument for the existence of God. This is true because, without God, the only explanation is that a cloud of hydrogen gas of unknown origin, through chance, evolved into a compact mass of highly organized and differentiated matter—the human brain—which, in the body of a person, is capable of contemplating the universe! One must decide which of the two faith alternatives is more reasonable: chance or intelligence.

The Phenomena of Sense Perception

By means of specialized sense organs, we perceive our environment through vision, hearing, equilibrium, taste, touch, and smell. However, seeing does not occur in the eye; taste does not occur on the tongue; feeling does not occur on the finger tips; and smell does not take place in the nose. All sense perceptions actually occur in the brain. As one touches a silky fabric or pricks his finger with a sharp object, nerve endings are stimulated. A biochemical nerve impulse is then transmitted by way of specialized neurons to the brain receptor where the sensation is interpreted as "soft and silky" or as "ouch."

Vision is the result of a sequence of events which is nothing less than phenomenal. Light rays bounce off the object that is "seen" and pass through the cornea, aqueous humor, lens, and vitreous humor of the eye where they are bent and focused onto the retina. By way of muscles, the eye can be rotated and the pupil dilated or constricted to regulate the amount of light falling on the retina. Muscles also cause light rays entering both eyes to converge onto the same area of the retina, forming one image instead of two.

The retina has rod and cone cells which contain photopigments that enable one to perceive not only shades of gray, but color as well. Rod cells contain a molecule which allows one to perceive shades of gray as the molecule changes structure. A human retina contains approximately 100 million rod cells. There are three types of cone cells which allow one to perceive each of the three primary colors. A human retina contains approximately three million cone cells.

The phenomenon we call vision does not occur when light falls upon the rods and cones. Cells in the rods and cones convert light energy into atomic motion, which then, by way of specialized nerve fibers, must be conducted to the brain. The conduction path proceeds through specialized components of the optic nerve. The exact nature of the biochemical process that occurs in the brain and finally generates the visual image remains unknown.

It is not significant that certain aspects of the visual process remain yet unexplained. Remember, the Christian's God is not a God of gaps in scientific knowledge. We hope and expect to learn more about the visual process. What *is* significant is that organisms are sensitive to their environment for a purpose. They were intelligently designed with that end in mind. All organisms—from simple bacterial cells to human beings— are sensitive to their environment. This remarkable design illustrates the fulfillment of purpose by God, the Master Designer.

Gravitation—Cosmic Glue

Isaac Newton was a devout believer in God. According to tradition, he discovered the Law of Universal Gravitation by pursuing the reason that an apple fell from a tree to the ground. Newton proceeded to show that every object in the universe has an attraction for every other object in the universe. It is as if every object is attached to every other object by an invisible elastic glue. The more massive the objects and the closer together they are, the stronger their attraction; the less massive and the farther apart, the weaker their attraction. Therefore, an object such as an apple falls toward the center of the earth because the earth has more mass than the apple. The earth pulls on the apple, and the apple pulls on the earth. Since the apple has less mass than the earth, it accelerates toward the earth and "falls."

Newton's Law is a fundamental principle that describes the physical universe. Einstein's theory of relativity necessitated only slight modifications of Newton's Law. The invisible, elastic, cosmic glue is real; gravitation can be described by precise mathematical statements. Although there is no known reason why the cosmic glue should exist, if it did not, the universe as we know it would be impossible. Consider the following examples of how the cosmic glue works.

At the mouth of the Rance River on the coast of Brittany, in France, are electrical power-generating dynamos driven by the tides that flow in and out of the Rance River estuary. Here the tide fluctuates forty-four feet daily, creating enough energy to provide electrical power to supply the needs of Brittany and regions beyond. But what is the power that drives the dynamos that generate the electricity? To say "it is the ebb and flow of the tide," is to answer the question superficially. The tides ebb and flow because the earth rotates on its axis. Gravity, the invisible cosmic glue which connects the earth and the moon, is relentlessly tugging at earth's oceans, shifting the tides in a night-and-day cycle. The homes and industries of Brittany are powered by the invisible cosmic force, gravitation!

An enormous rocket thrust was necessary to lift off the Apollo moon rocket because the opposing force of gravity had to be overcome. However, as the spaceship moved farther from the earth, the force of gravitational attraction between the earth and the spaceship became weaker and weaker. About one-tenth of the distance from the earth to the moon, the gravitational attraction of the earth for the spaceship became smaller than the gravitational attraction of the moon. The spaceship then began to be accelerated toward the moon. Upon leaving the moon, it required less power to blast off because the moon is less massive than the earth and, therefore, attracted the spaceship with less force.

On the return trip, the gravitational attraction of the moon for the spacecraft became weaker as it moved farther from the moon. Eventually, attraction by the moon became smaller than the earth's attraction, and the spacecraft began to accelerate the astronauts toward earth. The entire round trip from earth to the moon was made possible because of the existence of universal gravitation. Indeed, the planets, stars, and galaxies maintain their ever-shifting positions and relationships because of gravitation.

Is it not superficial to say that the homes and industries of Brittany are powered by gravity or that the spaceship was returned to earth by gravity? Is there not still a greater force that stands behind and sustains gravitational attraction? There is indeed! It is Christ, God's Son, for "He is before all things, and in him all things hold together" (Colossians 1:17). Christ, not gravity, is the universal cosmic glue that holds the universe together.

The Uniqueness of Water

A water molecule consists of two atoms of hydrogen and one atom of oxygen: it is a simple molecule. However, in terms of properties which it exhibits, water is complex. Approximately three-fourths of the surface of the earth is covered with water, and 60 to 90 percent of the total mass of many living things consists of this single chemical substance, H_2O. Although we cannot discuss all of them here, water has no less than twelve properties giving it uniqueness which makes life on earth possible.

Water has an unusual capacity to absorb, store, and distribute heat. At its most fundamental level, life in the cell consists of approximately 2,000 chemical reactions, each of which occurs with either the production or the consumption of heat. A life-support medium, therefore, must be extremely effective as a heat-transfer agent. Water is unusually effective in this respect.

Not only is this property of water important to the living cell, but also it is important to our planet. A drop of just a few degrees in the average temperature of the oceans would result in a new Ice Age over all the continents. Moisture circulating in the atmosphere serves to keep the earth from radiating too much heat in the winter and absorbing too much in the summer. Indeed, the earth is an "air-conditioned" planet.

The density of water changes with temperature in a manner different from all other naturally occurring substances. This unique property of water is significant because, as surface water freezes in rivers, ponds, lakes, and oceans, ice floats. The floating ice thus insulates marine life below it against freezing conditions. Even in regions of Antarctica, water in the liquid state, and therefore life, exists beneath several feet of ice. If the density of water changed with varying temperatures like other naturally occurring substances, rivers, ponds, lakes, and oceans would effectively freeze from bottom to top forcing marine life to the surface where it, too, would freeze and die.

Water exhibits an extremely high surface tension. Because of this property, it travels upward in defiance of gravity through tiny pores and capillaries in the trunks and stems of plants. Water molecules cohere to one another very strongly. The result is that, as water evaporates from leaf surfaces of even giant sequoias and redwoods, each evaporating molecule pulls another up behind it, thus providing continuous nourishment for the tree. This situation would not be possible if it were not for the high surface tension which water exhibits.

Water's molecular structure causes it to be a near-universal solvent. It is, therefore, suitable for dissolving a wide variety of chemical compounds, both organic and inorganic. Because of this property, water carries dissolved nutrients to all parts of both plant and animal organisms. For the same reason, it serves to dissolve waste products for removal from organisms.

The physical properties of water are not a happy coincidence. Water exhibits all the attributes of a molecule designed for the purposes it fulfills. The fact that the chemist can explain the unusual properties of water by reference to certain structural features does not negate our conclusion—simple water shows evidence of intelligent design!

Viruses, DNA, and a Single Cell

Viruses are not alive. They are too simple, chemically speaking, to exhibit properties, such as metabolism and reproduction, which are normally associated with living things. Viruses are, therefore, much simpler in composition than simple single-cell organisms. Likewise, single-cell organisms such as bacteria are much simpler than complex organisms such as man or animals.

Viruses consist largely of either the chemical substance DNA or RNA covered with a protein coat. The virus 0X174 is one of the simplest ever studied. It consists largely of DNA which is the molecule that carries encoded genetic material. In 1977 a landmark achievement was accomplished in the field of biochemistry: the complete chemical structure of the DNA molecule of 0X174 was determined. It consists of a total of 5,386 smaller molecules (which we shall designate by the letters A,C,G, and T) hooked to one another by a continuous sequence of chemical bonds.

By making letters smaller than those you are reading and by pushing them closer together, one could possibly get 5,386 letters on one page of this book. That one-page sequence of letters A,C,G, and T would represent the total genetic composition of the virus.

Comparatively speaking, bacteria are more complicated than viruses. *Escherichia coli* is an example of a common bacterium. It would take no less than 2,000 pages of the same letters A,C,G, and T in continuous sequence to represent the genetic sequence in one single cell of the bacterium *E. coli*. If even one letter were omitted, inserted, or exchanged with another letter during cell division, the result would be a mutation which would most likely be harmful to the cell.

That is only the beginning of the remarkable story of DNA. An adult person has approximately thirteen trillion (13,000,000,000,000) cells in his body. Each living cell, except for reproductive and red blood cells, contains exactly the same copy of DNA as all the other cells. In other words, one liver cell contains exactly the same sequence of A,C,G, and T in its forty-six chromosomes as a cell on the tip of one's nose. If the DNA in *any one* cell were represented by a continuous sequence of letters and printed on pages much larger than the pages of this book, the sequence would fill *every page of every volume of forty complete sets of Encyclopedia Britannica!*

A person receives one-half of the encoded genetic information from his mother and one-half from his father at the time the father's sperm cell fertilizes the mother's egg cell. Starting at that moment, all that genetic information is rapidly and faithfully copied as tissues are differentiated into all the organs of the body. To be sure, the Psalmist expressed it best when he said, "I am fearfully and wonderfully made" (Psalms 139:14 *KJV*). We might add that, not only are we fearfully and wonderfully *made*, but we are also fearfully and wonderfully *designed*. God knew what He was doing when He created life.

Hemoglobin—A Remarkable Oxygen Carrier

Within the sequence of letters A,C,G, and T of DNA resides encoded information which specifies precise sequences of amino acids which make up proteins. Proteins are fundamental structural molecules in the plant and animal kingdoms. They usually contain a continuous string of about 300 amino acids. Since only twenty amino acid building blocks exist, it is apparent that in protein structure some of the amino acids are used repeatedly. One sequence of amino acids may be found in human hair, another in wool, another in silk, another in a spider web, and so on.

A very interesting protein which is, in fact, four proteins functioning as a unit is human hemoglobin. Enclosed within each of the four protein units is a nonprotein organic molecule called a porphyrin. At the center of the porphyrin is an atom of iron. Oxygen binds to the iron and is thereby transported by hemoglobin from lung tissue to peripheral tissues. The hemoglobin molecule shows evidence of design in its ability to bind, transport, and release oxygen as needed.

One would suspect that if hemoglobin easily binds to oxygen, it would not easily release oxygen, thus making it useless as a molecule for transporting oxygen. However, the hemoglobin molecule is so constructed that it releases its oxygen upon demand from the cells.

For example, when one is working, he needs to consume large amounts of oxygen in peripheral tissue cells and so needs hemoglobin to deliver more oxygen. To accomplish this, cellular levels of certain acids and a chemical called 2,3-DPG increase. Increased cellular levels of these substances interact with hemoglobin bound to oxygen, causing it to release its oxygen at a faster rate.

Furthermore, a hemoglobin molecule contains a total of 574 amino acids. Slight alteration of the structure of the molecule by substitution or deletion of one amino acid for another may drastically alter the function of the molecule. For example, the substitution of only one amino acid for another in two of the four chains of hemoglobin results in the disease known as sickle-cell anemia. Hemoglobin displays all of the marks of having been architecturally designed for a particular function: oxygen transport and delivery.

Conclusion

Everything we see in nature teaches us to trust the Creator whom we cannot see. The entire spectrum of nature—from the microscopic world to the cosmic world—evidences the Creator's design. To be sure, God does not show Himself to us directly; He still wants us to walk by faith. Nevertheless, everywhere we turn we see clues which God left for us to conclude that He created and sustains all of reality. The vast amount of teleological evidence shouts in reason's ear, "God exists, and He has designed reality suitable for His purposes."

Ye fearful saints, fresh courage take,
The clouds ye so much dread,
Are big with mercy and shall break
In blessings on your head.

William Cowper

5

What Have I Done To Deserve This?

In Chapter 4 we emphasized the claim that God purposefully designed the world. The implication is that God designed the world *for man.* Perhaps the most formidable argument for the *nonexistence* of God is the claim that there appear to be many things in this world which are not in man's best interest. For example, what possible good can a pesky housefly serve? Much more seriously, why does evil exist in a world which we believe an all-powerful, all-good God created? Why are innocent children born handicapped for life with distressful congenital diseases? In the following two chapters we will address the problems of evil, sin, and suffering.

Evil and Suffering Are Two Different Problems

Man cannot answer questions about the origin of God. If we are to know anything about where God came from, God will have to tell us Himself. God has not chosen to reveal that information to us. Likewise, the origin of Satan has not been revealed. One can speculate endlessly about the origins of God and Satan. Some evidence suggests that Satan may be a fallen angel (Jude 6), but beyond that, little is known about him except that he is real and seeks to destroy what is good (1 Peter 5:8).

We should remember that we cannot expect to answer all questions we may have about the world in which we live—because we walk by faith and not by sight. There are certain things which will remain forever unknown to us. It is both a human and Christian virtue to patiently accept them as unknowns. One will find it helpful to memorize Isaiah 55:8: "For my thoughts are not your thoughts, neither are your ways my ways, says the Lord," and Deuteronomy 29:29: "The secret things belong to the Lord our God; but the things that are revealed belong to us and to our children for ever."

SIN OR EVIL RESULTS FROM MAN'S BAD CHOICES

The fact that babies experience suffering but are not capable of doing evil deeds is sufficient evidence for us to see that evil and suffering are two different problems. Evil, or sin, is entirely the result of bad choices. Babies cannot make bad choices; animals cannot make bad choices.

In the Garden of Eden, Adam and Eve had the choice of eating or not eating the forbidden fruit from the tree of knowledge of good and evil. The fact that God placed the tree before them was not an evil act on God's part. Sometimes we tend to blame God for giving us choices. Before we do so, however, we should consider the alternative to freedom of choice.

God did not have to give Adam and Eve the choice of eating or not eating the forbidden fruit. He could have made the decision for them. The result would have been that Adam and Eve, and mankind to follow, would have been deprived of free will. Had that been the case, Adam and Eve would have been little more than God's toy dolls repeating a recorded message whenever their strings were pulled. What kind of existence would that have been? It would not have been a meaningful existence at all; it would have been puppetry. Evil in the world is, therefore, the consequence of bad choices on man's part. It is unfortunate that we are inclined to focus on the fact that evil exists. Instead we should focus on God's response to man's evil choice to disobey Him.

God's Response to Man's Evil Choice

The true significance of the biblical story of Eden is not that Adam and Eve chose to do an evil thing. Had you or I been there, we would likely have done what they did. The significance of the story is God's response to their choice to disobey Him. I am not referring to God's punishment of Adam and Eve; what I am referring to is the unfolding of the story of a loving, benevolent Father.

God determined that, regardless of the price that He had to pay, He would make it possible for fallen man to return to His original spiritual relationship with Deity. Thus began God's pursuit which became the basis for the biblical plot. That pursuit develops throughout the Old Testament and ends at Calvary. The plot is God's pursuing man and making it possible for him, once again, to make the *right choice*, the choice to obey God.

Instead of blaming God for evil in the world, we should acknowledge that God has not caused evil and that He should not be blamed for man's evil choices. Rather we should recognize what God has done in response to man's evil. What God has done is allow Calvary. At Calvary, the blood of Deity, made fully man, dropped upon a sinful earth—sinful, not because of God who created it, but sinful because His creatures make wrong choices.

Since it was impossible for man, by his deeds, to undo the consequences of evil choices, the benevolent God who created him *did what man could not do*. God now says to us in effect, "You failed in Eden, but now you have another chance; accept my Son, and I will accept you back."

Someone may respond, "What about the person who makes wrong choices but who never has heard or never will hear about Calvary's love?" That is a good question. The most unfortunate fact of reality is that persons live and die without learning of God's pursuit of man. We must remember, however, that God knows every person who has ever lived better than a potter knows clay or better than a violin maker knows his instrument. Who is better equipped to fix a broken violin than the violin maker? God knows all about us. He knows our inclination to lust and our temptation to disobey. Furthermore, He has placed within the mind of every man, woman, and responsible child a moral law which He expects us to honor.

49

CHRIST
IS GOD'S RESPONSE TO MAN'S EVIL CHOICES

Before Calvary, it was possible for man to live a life pleasing to God. Noah, Job, and Abraham are notable examples of persons who generally did so. However, without Christ, no person could be forgiven of sins, not even Noah, Job and Abraham—but Calvary has made that possible. God, through Christ, will judge every person, and we can be sure that He will not make mistakes in doing so. However, a person who does not know and obey Christ cannot enjoy freedom from the power of sin and evil. Christ's disciples must take this message to a sinful world!

Sin and Suffering May Be Related

Man is always responsible for his own bad choices. God does not hold a person responsible for bad choices made by another person. However, my suffering may be directly related to either my bad choices or to the bad choices of another person. Sin and suffering, therefore, *may* be related, but they are not *necessarily* related.

As an example, Fetal Alcohol Syndrome is a condition in which a child may experience mental retardation, as well as other abnormal symptoms, because his mother drank alcoholic beverages during pregnancy. Ethyl alcohol, the kind of alcohol in beer, wine, and liquor, is a toxic chemical substance. To a point, an adult is able to detoxify ethyl alcohol if his liver is healthy because the liver is the organ that recognizes and detoxifies substances foreign to the body.

Eventually alcohol consumption leads to irreversible damage to liver, brain, and nerve tissue cells. A developing fetus, however, is incapable of effectively detoxifying ethyl alcohol. If a mother consumes alcohol during the early stages of pregnancy, severe and irreversible damage can be done to the developing fetus. The result is Fetal Alcohol Syndrome. In this instance, retardation of the child is the direct result of bad choices—not bad choices of the child, but of the mother. The child is the innocent victim.

A second example of the connection between sin and suffering is the Acquired Immunodeficiency Syndrome. AIDS is a viral disease that is most commonly spread through homosexual activity, sexual behavior that God has condemned. It is a horribly debilitating and wasteful disease. Adults who do not receive contaminated blood in a transfusion, who do not use AIDS-contaminated needles or other instruments, and who do not engage in sexual activity with AIDS-infected persons are not in danger of infection. However, one who chooses to engage in risky behavior may be forced to accept devastating consequences of an evil decision. Therefore, sin and suffering may be directly related. The person who makes an evil choice may, in this life, suffer the consequences of his own evil behavior. The spread of AIDS is not God's seeking vengeance in retribution. It is an unfortunate example of a consequence man may pay for acting against God's physical and biological laws.

Other well-known examples of physical suffering which occur because bad choices are made include: lung or mouth cancer due to smoking cigarettes, chewing tobacco, or dipping snuff; sclerosis of the liver due to excessive alcohol consumption; venereal disease which is often contracted due to promiscuous sexual behavior; and a vast array of symptoms resulting from indulgence in drugs such as marijuana and cocaine.

Sin and Suffering Are Not Necessarily Related

The Deuteronomic Code is given in Deuteronomy 12 through 26. In summary, the Deuteronomic Code was God's basis for delivering Israel: "Do good, and you will be blessed; do evil and you will suffer." This code was, and continues to be, a generally true principle: doing good will result in our being blessed, and doing evil will result in our suffering. However, the fact that this is a generally true principle does not mean that those who do good will *never* suffer. And it does *not* mean that if one suffers he has necessarily sinned.

It was common in Jesus' day, and it is common today, for persons to associate sin and suffering. How frequently do we hear, in response to personal tragedy, "What have I done to deserve this?" However, the world in which we live is not a world of retribution; that is, there is no necessary association between suffering and sin *in this world*. We live in a world in which good and evil are mingled. In the world to come, however, good will be rewarded and evil punished.

Christ teaches us to understand that *this* world is not a world of physical retribution. God makes "his sun rise on the evil and on the good, and sends rain on the just and on the unjust" (Matthew 5:45). This principle, which Christ gives in the Sermon on the Mount, also applies to physical suffering; like the rain, pain falls on the just and on the unjust.

Luke and John relate significant stories about Christ which address the relationship between sin and suffering. Luke relates a story of persons who told Jesus that Pilate's henchmen had slain some Galileans who were in the act of offering sacrifices. Apparently this act occurred in the Gentile court of the temple in Jerusalem. Galileans were typically a crude people, and evidently, without provocation, Pilate had had some of them slain. The manner in which the people interpreted this event disturbed Christ.

The people concluded that the slain persons must have committed secret sins and "were worse sinners than all the other Galileans because they suffered thus" (Luke 13:2). In other words, by misapplying the Deuteronomic Code, the people thought that God had given the slain Galileans what they deserved. Jesus' response to this popular conclusion was, "No, but unless you repent, you will all likewise perish." The lesson to be gained from the horrible incident of the slain Galileans is *not* that we live in a world of retribution. The lesson *is* that when we die we must be ready for the retribution that awaits us in the world to come.

In the same text, Luke tells of Jesus addressing the similar problem of eighteen persons who perished apparently because they were innocently standing beneath a tower which fell on them. Such tragic events still happen today. Innocent persons are struck by lightning, and drunk drivers cross into the lanes of innocent people. The people Jesus spoke to interpreted the tower disaster to mean that those killed were "worse offenders than all the others who dwelt in Jerusalem" (Luke 13:4). Again, Jesus responded, "No, but unless you repent you will all likewise perish." Retribution is coming, but it is not in this world.

It is clear from the story of the blind man in John 9 that the common Jewish belief in Jesus' day was that sickness or suffering was necessarily related to sin. Working on the assumption that where there is suffering, there must be sin, Jesus' disciples asked regarding the blind man, "Rabbi, who sinned, this man or his parents, that he was born blind?" To Jesus' puzzled inquirers the association between sin and suffering was apparent—someone had sinned, or else the man would not have been born blind. Furthermore, the people thought the blind man had either committed a prenatal sin or inherited sin from his parents. This man represented a philosophical dilemma. To the amazement of the inquirers, Jesus responded by saying, "It was not that this man sinned, or his parents, but that the works of God might be made manifest in him" (v. 3). Jesus again disclaimed any necessary connection between sin and suffering.

Some modern interpreters have concluded that when Jesus stated "that the works of God might be made manifest" in the blind man, He was claiming that God *had caused* the man to be born blind so that he might be cured by Jesus. This interpretation is as much a mistake as the one the Jewish community originally made regarding the connection between sin and suffering. Many other blind people were in Jerusalem, and Jesus did not heal them all. God may have *allowed* the man to be born blind, but God did not *cause* him to be born blind. God allows tragedy, but God does not cause tragedy. It is contrary to God's nature for Him either to cause tragedy or to rejoice in misfortune or tragedy.

Is Physical Pain Friend or Foe?

The Bible does not teach that Adam and Eve were free from pain prior to their sins. Pain is a consequence of our being sensitive to our environment. We might expect that, if Adam had stubbed his toe while selecting a fragrant rose for Eve, he would have felt the impact and perhaps responded with an "ouch." After the fall, God, in issuing punishment to Eve said, "I will *greatly multiply* your pain in childbearing" (Genesis 3:16), thus implying that she had previously experienced the sensation of pain and possibly even pain in childbearing. (We have no definite biblical claim that Cain was her first child.)

Pain and pleasure are opposing sensations associated with the physical sense we call "touch" or "feeling." In Chapter 4, we offered the existence of the physical senses as evidence of purposeful design by a benevolent God. It is impossible for us to be sensitive to our environment and, at the same time, unaware of the unpleasant sensation called pain. Mountains are not possible without valleys; pleasure opens the possiblility of pain. Sensitivity is an essential characteristic of being "alive." More than that, the experiences of pleasure and pain are essential characteristics that give life quality: life without any sensitivity would be little more than a vegetative existence.

To demonstrate that pain is friend rather than foe, consider the following example. A friend of mine lost all sensation of pain in one of his legs. On a cold winter night, to provide warmth for circulation, he wrapped his leg in an electric blanket. During the night, an electrical short developed in the blanket, and his leg was so severely burned that it became infected and had to be amputated. Unfortunately, the amputation did not remove all of the toxins from the infection, and my friend died. Had he felt at least some sensation of pain, he would have had a warning that he was being burned. In this case, was pain intended to be friend or foe?

Pain is not neurologically, biologically, psychologically, or chemically understood. However, recent discoveries have shed significant light on processes by which we experience pain. A major discovery in medicinal chemistry has been the discovery of a new class of compounds called the *endorphins* which have also been called "the body's natural morphine." We have long known that morphine produces euphoria and a lessening of the sensation of pain. In fact, morphine is one of our most powerful analgesics. Researchers began to study the reason why morphine exhibits the effect it has on the human body. They concluded that since morphine is not a natural body chemical, a yet-undiscovered natural substance might be produced by the body in order to compensate for pain.

Scientists began searching for the mystery compound. In 1975 they discovered a morphine-like class of compounds produced by the body which they named endorphins. We now know that endorphins are produced by the body during times of stress. Apparently, their purpose is to help us deal with the problem of pain. For example, endorphin blood levels increase for long-distance runners on even an easy run, but the endorphin blood levels for a woman in childbirth are elevated approximately ten times higher than those of the long distance runner! The presence of the endorphins helps to explain the feeling of euphoria after the completion of a stressful event such as strenuous exercise.

For many decades we did not know how common aspirin works to alleviate pain or to reduce fever. Within the last few years, scientists have discovered another new class of compounds which the body makes, called the *prostaglandins*. The body makes these compounds to tell us that something is wrong. Aspirin apparently interferes with the synthesis of prostaglandins, thereby interrupting the message and reducing or removing the sensation of pain. The fact that our bodies are so designed to tell us in this way that something is wrong is nothing short of remarkable.

Conclusion

It is indeed unfortunate that some persons endure excruciating pain for years. However, we have seen that the condition of humanity would be much worse in the absence of pain. We have also seen that our Creator understood the problems that pain would present to us and has given us means by which we can deal with pain and even raise our tolerance of pain.

Explaining the problems of pain, suffering, and sin intellectually is one thing. Accepting the implications of what we know and internalizing that information as we experience suffering is more difficult. However, God has also given us His promise: "He will not let you be tempted beyond your strength, but with the temptation will also provide the way of escape, that you may be able to endure it" (1 Corinthians 10:13).

Judge not the Lord by feeble sense,
But trust Him for His grace;
Behind a frowning providence,
He hides a smiling face.
                    William Cowper

6

Why Must
The Innocent Suffer?

I had a friend in graduate school who said that he would never believe in God. He reasoned, "I worked in Children's Hospital, and I cannot believe in a God who allows innocent children to suffer as I have seen them suffer." His philosophical eye had caught the suffering of the children, but he did not take equal note of the compassion of the doctors, nurses, and support staff at the hospital.

Nevertheless, I judged my friend to be a sincere person who spoke from the heart. His reasoning was that if God exists and He is both all-good and all-powerful, if He wished, He could do something about the suffering of innocent people. He reasoned further that since God does not do anything, He either does not wish to do anything—in which case He is not all-good—or He cannot do anything—in which case He is not all-powerful. To take away either God's goodness or His power is to effectively deny God's existence.

Do you see anything wrong with my friend's reasoning? I did not realize it at the time, but he was expressing the strongest argument that atheists have for the nonexistence of God—the suffering of innocent people. Although the suffering of the innocent is a difficult fact of life to accept, his reasoning has fundamental flaws.

First, the argument assumes that, somehow, God is responsible because He does not intervene and disallow suffering. Second, the argument supposes that no good can come from suffering. Third, the argument assumes that God has done nothing about the problem and He continues to do nothing. Finally, the argument assumes we should understand the role of suffering as clearly as God understands it. Each of the flaws in my friend's reasoning will be addressed in this chapter.

The problem of the suffering of innocent people is most difficult. It has challenged and perplexed the minds of common men, philosophers, and theologians for centuries. The problem *is* *answerable* academically and intellectually. However, because it can be answered academically does not mean it can be answered emotionally.

I may know in my mind that it is necessary for innocent people to suffer. That does not mean, however, that when suffering comes, I will not cry out with the believers of all ages, "Oh God, why does this have to happen to me?" Intellectual argument will not be adequate then; what I need in the midst of suffering is a faith by which I can both live and die.

Is God Responsible For the Suffering of the Innocent?

This question has both a "yes" and "no" answer. Yes, God is responsible because He elected to create man as a creature sensitive to his environment. The problem would never have existed in the first place had man not been created a sensitive creature. However, sensitivity allows both pain *and* pleasure. If there is to be pleasure, there must be the possibility of pain. But does that strike at God's omnipotence? No, not at all. All things that are intrinsically possible are possible with God (Jeremiah 32:27, Matthew 19:26). However, *some* things are intrinsically impossible. For example, mountains are not possible without valleys; it is impossible for God to lie; flesh is no match for steel when they impact at sixty miles per hour; pleasure opens the possiblility of pain.

God is also responsible for the innocent suffering because, as an all-powerful God, He could have created us so that we suffer in direct proportion to our actions. But is that what we want? No, we do not want what we deserve; we want mercy and grace. In a world where choices are possible, what penalty would you assess for an angry word, a lustful eye, an ungrateful attitude, an abusive father, an abandoning mother, a seductive woman, or a provoked murderer? The Mosaic principle of "an eye for an eye and a tooth for a tooth" was plausible, but it was difficult to apply.

Would you like to live in a world where an omnipotent God immediately served retribution for bad choices? Not at all! We would rather choose to live in a world where there is a second chance. That is the kind of world God has given us.

There is also a "no" response to the question: "Is God responsible for the suffering of innocent people?" That response is discussed in the remainder of the chapter.

Is It Always God's Will?

We once had a neighbor whose faith I greatly admired. I doubt that I have ever known anyone who believed with such intensity of feeling that absolutely everything that happens is God's will. I do not think the words "chance" or "accident" were in her vocabulary. I would not write this section with the intention of offending anyone. It is not true that every occurrence is God's will. Many things—but not all things—occur because of the will of God. However, some things occur because of man's will, not God's.

God created man with a will by which he is to conduct his own affairs. If man chooses to turn his face toward heaven and curse God, he can do that. One may spit at God if he wishes, but God will not spit back. God demonstrated that at Calvary. He will not respond with retribution in this world. If a person wills to drink alcoholic beverages until he can no longer drive safely and then crosses the road and kills an innocent child, we should not respond by saying, "It is God's will." God did not will that the man take the drink or that the accident occur. Man's will often violates God's will.

Furthermore, we should not blame God or hold Him responsible when a child is born with a congenital disease. It is God's will that biological laws which govern cell division exist, but it is not God's will that any child or parent suffer due to birth defects. In Chapter 3 we noted the remarkable complexity of human genetic material and the sometimes disastrous consequences of genetic mutations which appear to occur at random. What we did not note is that approximately 2,000 birth defects are known which give rise to congenital disorders. Many are due to mutations which occur during cell division. Even more compelling is the fact that many times that number of birth defects are not known, and the wonder of wonders is that fertilization, cell division, differentiation, and birth occur successfully at all!

Perhaps the most remarkable of all enzymes is DNA polymerase which is responsible for replicating DNA, a process which must occur before cell division can take place. Not only does DNA polymerase synthesize new genetic material but also, after it has accomplished the synthesis, it scans its work—looking for certain kinds of errors! Once it finds an error, it removes it and corrects it. Although cell division may occur in minutes, it takes DNA polymerase as long as twenty hours to correct certain errors. Rather than living in a world governed by a hateful, spiteful God, we live in a world where the Creator has evidenced His love for His creatures by the laws He has imposed.

God created physical and biological law, and He has decreed that all things within His physical universe be controlled by those laws. That does not mean that God is responsible, or that it is God's will, if brakes fail on a school bus and disaster occurs on a class outing. It is God's will that we check our brakes, drive within speed limits, use good judgment, and arrive home safely.

Christ prayed, "Thy will be done on earth as it is in heaven" (Matthew 6:10). His prayer was that man's will be brought under submission to God's will and that man do God's will on earth even as the angels in Heaven. We may sometimes find it difficult to know whether an occurrence is the result of man's will, God's will, or even Satan's will. However, it will be helpful to remember that while God's will always seeks what is good, Satan's will seeks what is evil. Man's will may seek either good or evil. My task is to strive constantly to bring my will into subjection to God's will. Each day my prayer should be, "Not my will but Thine be done."

Do We Then Believe in Answered Prayer?

Do we then believe in answered prayer? To this question I hasten to respond, "Most definitely I believe in answered prayer, and I hope you do, too." If I have a personal proof for the existence of God, it is not the arguments from reason or nature; it is that God has answered my prayers and directed my life. One may observe that this is personal and possibly even subjective. To this I respond, "It is nevertheless real to me." I do not expect to convince an atheist that God exists by testifying of my personal experiences. Yet in my heart I know what I know. What I do not know is *how God answers prayer.*

Remember that one's relationship to God is the relationship of clay to its potter. I do not expect to understand how God answers prayer any more than I expect to understand how He created the universe. I can endlessly theorize about how God answers prayer, but in the end, I will not know. I do know that it is God's will that I pray to Him and even be persistent in prayer.

The Apostle Paul prayed three times for God to remove the thorn in his flesh. We do not know what the thorn was, but it was most likely some form of physical suffering. We do not assume that Paul's prayers were casually spoken requests. Rather we assume that Paul prayed fervently to God and pleaded that his adversity be taken away. God did not respond as Paul wished, but God did respond, saying, "My grace is sufficient for you, for my power is made perfect in weakness" (2 Corinthians 12:9). Paul's prayer was not an unanswered prayer; it was answered.

It is important for one to understand that such a position as I have just taken is *not* a deistic treatment of the problem of the suffering innocent. Deism holds that God is completely removed from His creation: like a watchmaker and one of his products, God has wound up the universe, walked away, and left it to run on its own. Nothing is more foreign to my concept of God than the suggestion that He is not a participant in reality. However, it is necessary for us to acknowledge that on occasion we are subject to the whims of nature. It is not always the fastest runner who wins the race, the strongest who wins the battle, or the intelligent and wise who prosper—as was observed centuries ago by the Preacher:

Again I saw that under the sun the race is not to the swift, nor the battle to the strong, nor bread to the wise, nor riches to the intelligent, nor favor to the men of skill; but *time and chance happen to them all*. For man does not know his time. Like fish which are taken in an evil net, and like birds which are caught in a snare, so the sons of men are snared at an evil time, when it suddenly falls upon them. Ecclesiastes 9:11, 12

As difficult as it may be, it is necessary for us to recognize a truth claimed in the above passage, "Time and chance happen to all." Admitting this does not mean believing that God is unconcerned and is removed from reality. Rather, it means that God has willed that human activity be affected by time and chance. Because God is all-powerful, He can overrule as He so desires. Because He is transcendent, He can even overrule without our awareness of His intervention. Again, it is the role of the Christian to be submissive to God's will and to pray, "Not my will but thine be done."

Is Hell Compatible With the Nature of God?

When Christ chose a word to describe the place of retribution for unforgiven sins committed in this life, He chose the word *gehenna* which means "the valley of Hinnom." The valley of Hinnom was the Jerusalem garbage dump where, typical of such places, "the worm does not die and fire is not quenched." As awful as the thought is, Hell is not only compatible with the nature of God; it is necessitated by His nature. If man does not receive retribution for sins in this life, justice requires that he receive punishment in the life to come. The biblical doctrine of God would be incomplete without a biblical doctrine of Hell.

It would be contrary to the nature of a benevolent God to send any soul to Hell. But God does not send anyone to Hell. By our choices in this life we, not God, determine whether we will be with God or separate from God in eternity. Each person repeats the drama of Eden every day by deciding whether to obey God. God has given a written law which must be obeyed. He has also given every person a moral law which must not be violated. God's pursuit of man from Eden to Calvary demonstrates that God does not want a single person to be lost.

God's word teaches that there will be a judgment (Hebrews 9:27). Each person will be judged by his words (Matthew 12:36, 37) and his works (Revelation 20:13). It is significant that God has delegated the task of judging to Christ (John 5:22). In fact, Christ will not only pronounce judgment; He will be the Christian's advocate to plead his case (1 John 2:1). What an advantage for the Christian—his judge is his defense attorney!

Job Had the Solution but Did Not Know It!

Many authorities recognize the book of Job as the oldest book in the Bible. It most likely belongs to the patriarchal period and is a magnificent piece of inspired literature. Scholars all over the world recognize it for its literary excellence whether or not they accept the remainder of the Bible. Because of the antiquity of the book of Job, we sense that man has always struggled with the problem of the suffering of innocent persons. The book also tells us that man has always known the solution to the problem of human suffering—just as Job knew it. Like Job, other men have been slow to recognize the solution. I strongly recommend that you stop here and read the book of Job. What follows is not a detailed analysis of the book but a brief synopsis.

Job was blameless and upright; he feared God and turned away from evil. Nevertheless, God allowed terrible calamities to fall upon him. Satan's claims were that God had built a hedge of protection around Job and that Job would curse God if his prosperity were taken away. In response to this accusation, God allowed Satan to have free course with Job, except that Satan was to spare Job's life.

Job was a wealthy man with sons and daughters. His children began to experience calamity after calamity. They were ravaged by raids, fire, and theft. A great wind, possibly a tornado, killed all of them. Only a servant escaped to carry the bad news to Job. The writer of Job observes, "In all this Job did not sin or charge God with wrong" (Job 1:22). Satan was then allowed to lift his hand against Job's person, and Job became afflicted with loathsome sores from the soles of his feet to the crown of his head. He sat in ashes for comfort and scraped the sores with a broken piece of pottery.

At this point, the drama of the Book of Job really begins, for here Job begins to struggle with the problem of suffering. When Job lived, many people believed—as some do today—that retribution, or Divine payment for sins, occurs in this life. In other words, where there is suffering, there must be sin. Job's wife believed so and told Job to "Curse God, and die" (Job 2:9). Job's response to his wife reflected the stance he was to maintain throughout his suffering: "Shall we accept good from God, and not trouble?" (Job 2:10, *NIV*) Job was then visited by three friends, Eliphaz, Bildad, and Zophar, who sat with him on the ground for three days without saying a word as they watched him suffer. Sometimes we who sympathize cannot find words to express our feelings for the sufferer, and, as was the case with Job's friends, when we speak, we may say the wrong thing.

Job broke the silence and cursed the day he was born. He wished he had died at birth or that he had been aborted (Job 3:1-16). As Job's friends began to speak, they did not have words of comfort but words of accusation. Eliphaz implored Job to admit his secret sins and turn to God, but Job stood steadfast and declared his innocence. Job called for evidence that he had sinned in proportion to his suffering and pleaded to speak directly to God. Bildad accused him of hypocrisy, asking, "Does God pervert justice?" and claimed that Job's children had received just payment for their transgressions. He again asked Job to repent, but Job challenged the popular belief that retribution for sins occurs in this life (Job 8:1-4; 9:22).

Job's third friend, Zophar, was tactless, caustic, and bitter as he told Job that he really deserved worse punishment than God had given him. Zophar also called Job to repentance, but Job responded by claiming that he was just as smart as Zophar (Job 12:1). Job called his friends who brought no comfort "worthless physicians," and asked them to keep silent. He again pleaded to speak directly with God so that he could argue his case (Job 13:3-5). It was in the midst of expressing deep resentment for his "comforters" who brought no comfort that Job expressed the solution to the problem of the suffering of the innocent: "Though he slay me, yet will I trust in him" (Job 13:15, *KJV*).

Job knew he was innocent; he knew he would be vindicated. He did not know why he was suffering, but he knew God was not punishing him for his sins. Job, therefore, *trusted in God*. The drama of Job could have ended there, but it did not. His friends presented two additional cycles of accusing speeches. Job continued to plead for an audience with God, and finally God condescended to speak with Job.

God's speech is found in Job 38. God asked Job approximately forty questions which highlighted Job's lack of understanding of everyday occurrences. Job sat humbled in sackcloth and ashes and understood what we must all understand if we are going to effectively deal with the problem of suffering in the world: *we must accept suffering in trusting faith just as we accept the other mysteries of life*. Job then understood and repented, not of sins he had committed but of his failure to understand:

> Then Job answered the Lord;
>   "I know that thou canst do all things,
>   and that no purpose of thine can be thwarted.
>   Who is this that hides counsel without knowledge?
>   Therefore I have uttered what I did not understand,
>   things too wonderful for me, which I did not know."
>   Job 42:1-3

Suffering Is a Part of God's Design

In Chapter 4 we presented evidence that this world has been purposefully designed by God for man. The atheist responds by claiming that such a position cannot be true and points to evil and suffering as evidence of chaos rather than design. As bad as it may seem, at times, this world is the best of all possible worlds for man to prepare for the world to come. God knew what He was doing.

God knew that Adam and Eve, and all of the rest of us, would choose to disobey, so He created a world of second chances and pursued us all the way to Calvary to make sure that we understand. God knew that we would experience suffering. He even knew that when Christ came to live among us for thirty-three years, He would experience the most horrible kind of suffering. Suffering in the world is neither an accident of God nor is it an afterthought. God carefully thought through implications of this reality *before* He created man (Acts 2:23).

We do not live in a world where there is retribution for sins committed. It is unmistakable that suffering was meant for our good. The Apostle Paul saw all of his suffering as "slight" and "momentary" (2 Corinthians 4:17), yet he suffered to the point that he was "utterly, unbearably crushed so that he despaired of life itself." In suffering, however, Paul saw God's purpose; it was "to make us rely not on ourselves but on God who raises the dead" (2 Corinthians 1:8, 9). One must achieve Christian maturity and the ability to see reality through the eyes of Christ to accept suffering in this way.

I sat talking with an elderly man who was dying of cancer. He had been a Christian just a few years. He understood that the disease was not reversible. He had exhausted every means of medical treatment, including cobalt radiation therapy. We talked plainly of death and of the fact that our trust is not in cobalt but in God who created the cobalt. He responded, "There is no one else to trust." That is the solution! Only through the eye of Christian faith can we state with Paul, "I consider that the sufferings of this present time are not worth comparing with the glory that is to be revealed to us" (Romans 8:18).

The tragedy is not that men suffer. The tragedy is that not all men know Christ who *helps* us in our suffering. Through Christ, we do not have hope merely in the "by and by," but we have hope in the "here and now." Romans 8:28 is a treasured text: "We know that in everything God works for good with those who love him, who are called according to his purpose." This text does not say that a school bus wreck which takes the lives of innocent children is good, or that birth defects are good, or that suffering is good, or that death is good. They are not good, and God does not rejoice in them. He does not cause these things to happen, but, in all these things, He works for our good. *God uses suffering purposefully.* God does not save us from suffering; He saves us in the midst of suffering.

Conclusion

Enduring affliction has a way of giving man a perspective on the meaning of life which he cannot get through any other experience. I have before me an article about a young man, Scott Schneider of Houston, Texas, who is afflicted with muscular dystrophy. Scott falls down, on the average, twice a day, 365 days a year. Yet he is a champion wheelchair athlete, "a world-class human being."[1] Scott considers muscular dystrophy his enemy—but also his *ally*. He says,

> If I had to do it all over again, and I made out a check list, I would check to be perfectly healthy. But in a real sense, I think I'm very lucky having MD. It has caused me not to take things for granted, to live life to the fullest. I don't know how I would have turned out if I didn't have muscular dystrophy. I might have been a real jerk.[2]

Take careful note of Scott's last words. His judgment is that it is better to be afflicted with the horrible disease of muscular dystrophy than to live as a "real jerk." Jerks of the world, take notice, for Scott Schneider has spoken truth and wisdom.

Thou didst make him for a little while lower than the angels,
Thou hast crowned him with glory and honor,
putting everything in subjection under his feet.

Hebrews 2:7, 8a

7

Was Jesus Really A Man?

The name "Jesus" establishes Christ as a person in history. He was a contemporary of persons we read about in secular history: Herod the Great, Herod Agrippa, Pontius Pilate, Tiberius Caesar, Felix, and Festus. Although the name "Jesus" means "savior" (Matthew 1:21), it was still a common name. Many boys and men in Palestine were named Jesus.

The word "Christ" means "anointed one" and affirms His Divinity. To distinguish Jesus the Christ from other men with the same name, Christ was called "Jesus of Nazareth" (Acts 2:22, 3:6). In referring to Himself, Christ frequently used the title "Son of Man." However, He did not intend to affirm His humanity by using this title. He most likely intended to identify Himself with the Son of Man in Old Testament prophecy (Daniel 7:13).

At one time liberal scholarship questioned that Jesus Christ was actually an authentic, historical person. Some people claimed He was a legend, a figment of overactive imaginations. However, such claims no longer survive in circles of responsible scholarship. That Jesus of Nazareth actually lived has been firmly established.

It is not my intention here to overemphasize the humanity of Jesus. However, His humanity may be as great a challenge to one's faith as His Deity. In fact, it is perhaps easier mentally to accept the idea that Jesus was *different from us* than it is to acknowledge that *in every respect He was like us.* The human nature of Jesus is just as essential to the biblical doctrine of Christ as His Divine nature is. One theme of the book of Hebrews is that we have a high priest in Heaven who understands our feelings, our hurts, and our sufferings (Hebrews

7:24, 25). Since Jesus was in all respects like we are, He can now intercede for us before God.

Jesus grew up in the obscure village of Nazareth, Galilee. The city of His birth, Bethlehem, was also insignificant at the time of His life on earth. He learned to read and write and developed the habit of worship at the synagogue. We assume that, as a teen-ager, He experienced the frustrations that teen-agers typically experience. He learned the carpenter's trade; He probably made plows, yokes, boats, furniture, and houses and possibly carved wooden objects.

Toward the end of the first century, men began to teach that Jesus had come in the spirit *but not in the flesh*. John was one of the few remaining apostles, and he effectively opposed this doctrine in his Gospel and letters. In his Gospel he states, "The Word became flesh" (John 1:14). Later John writes, "[which] we have heard, [which] we have seen with our eyes, [which] we have looked upon and touched with our hands, concerning the word of life" (1 John 1:1). John, therefore, affirms both the humanity and Divinity of Jesus.

The Witness of Secular History

Both Franklin D. Roosevelt and famed baseball player Babe Ruth were alive when I was a small child. I seem to recall hearing President Roosevelt make speeches over the radio, and I have frequently heard my parents speak of his presidency. But I never saw Babe Ruth hit a home run. However, with a bit of imagination, I can almost hear the crack of the bat against the ball as I recall my father describing Babe Ruth's slamming home runs over the fence of the old Sulfur Dell baseball park in Nashville, Tennessee. I mention these illustrations to point out that Josephus, one of the greatest Jewish historians, was born shortly after the death of Christ. His parents had been contemporaries of Christ, and he, no doubt, had heard them speak of Jesus just as I heard my father speak of Babe Ruth.

Josephus was not a follower of Christ. The following quotation, which contains a reference to Jesus, is found in Josephus' *Antiquities*, Book 18, chapter III:

At that time lived Jesus, a wise man, if he may be called a man: for he performed many wonderful works. He was a teacher of such men as received the truth with pleasure. He drew over to him many Jews and Gentiles. This was the Christ, and when Pilate, at the instigation of the chief men among us, had condemned him to the cross, they who had before conceived an affection for him did not cease to adhere to him. For on the third day he appeared to them alive again, the divine prophets having foretold these and many other wonderful things concerning him. And the sect of the Christians, so called from him subsists at this time.[1]

Although the above quotation from Josephus is found in the fourth-century writings of Eusebius, many modern scholars have concluded that an unbelieving Jew could not have stated "he was the Christ." In fact, Josephus believed that Vespasian was the Messiah. It is not seriously questioned that Josephus alludes to the historical Jesus; it is seriously questioned as to exactly what he said. On the Josephus quotation, F. F. Bruce states: "But a case can be made out for the view that the paragraph preserves a genuine reference to Christ by Josephus, which has, however, been subjected to modification by Christian scribes."[2] Bruce also notes, as should we, that it is not on the authority of Josephus that Christians believe in Christ![3]

In Acts 18, Luke states that Aquila and Priscilla, natives of Pontus, had recently come to Corinth from Rome because of Jewish persecution. The persecution to which Luke refers occurred during the reign of the emperor Claudius, A.D. 49-50. Bruce tells of a Roman author by the name of Suetonius, about A.D. 120, who wrote a biography of Claudius in which he refers to the Jewish persecution under Claudius. Suetonius states:

He expelled the Jews from Rome, on account of the riots in which they were constantly indulging, at the instigation of Chrestus [Christ]. (qtd. in Bruce)[4]

Bruce also describes Thallus, a Gentile historian, who wrote about A.D. 52 and is mentioned by Josephus in his *Antiquities*. Thallus curiously refers to the darkness which occurred during the crucifixion of Jesus and attributes it to an eclipse, saying, "The darkness was due to an eclipse of the sun" (qtd. in Bruce).[5] Julius Africanus, also mentioned by Bruce, was a Christian writer of the third century who quotes Thallus and discounts his claim that an eclipse had occurred. Julius argues that a full moon prevailed at the time of Passover when Jesus was crucified; therefore, an eclipse had not been possible (Bruce).[6]

Cornelius Tacitus, of about A.D. 117, was one of the early Roman historians. He had no sympathy for Christians. In recording the history of the reign of Nero, he gives the following account of the fire which destroyed Rome in A.D. 64 and Nero's attempt to shift the blame onto Christians:

> Christus [Christ] suffered the extreme penalty during the reign of Tiberius at the hands of one of our procurators, Pontius Pilatus, and a most mischievous superstition, thus checked for the moment, again broke out not only in Judea, the first source of the evil, but even in Rome, where all things hideous and shameful from every part of the world find their centre and become popular. . . .Covered with the skins of beasts, they were torn by dogs and perished, or were nailed to crosses or were doomed to the flames and burnt, to serve as a nightly illumination when daylight had expired.[7]

Tacitus clearly makes reference to the crucifixion of Christ in stating that Christ experienced "extreme penalty" at the hands of Pilate under Tiberius Caesar. The uncomplimentary portrayal of Christianity as a "mischievous superstition" is not surprising. The description of the immorality of Rome is accurate, and the reference to the mutilation of Christians is possibly a description of the way Christians were tortured in coliseums for sport.

Pliny the Younger served as Governor of Bithynia in Asia Minor. He wrote a letter about A.D. 112 to the emperor Trajan asking advice on how to deal with the Christians. In his letter he expressed bias against Christians. Nevertheless, he gave valuable testimony to the historical conduct and allegiance of early Christians.

> They affirmed, however, the whole of their guilt, or their error, was, that they were in the habit of meeting on a certain fixed day before it was light, when they sang in alternate verses a hymn to Christ, as to God, and bound themselves by a solemn oath, not to do any wicked deeds, but never to commit any fraud, theft or adultery, never to falsify their word, nor deny a trust when they should be called upon to deliver it up; after which it was their custom to separate, and then reassemble to partake of food—but food of an ordinary and innocent kind.[8]

Pliny's account of the worship habits of the early Christians is inspiring. The "fixed day" to which he alludes is, of course, Sunday. A possible reason why early Christians met before daybreak was to avoid persecution. Frequently they met among the catacombs and sang their songs quietly to keep from attracting attention. The food to which he alludes is surely the Lord's Supper. As they partook, they rededicated themselves to living according to the moral standards of Christ.

Lucian was a Greek satirist and public speaker of the second century. In the following statement mentioned by M. C. Tenney, Lucian alludes to Christ, the brotherhood of Christians, the refusal of Christians to worship Greek gods, and Christian worship of Christ:

> ...the man who was crucified in Palestine because he introduced this new cult into the world....Furthermore, their first lawgiver persuaded them that they are all brothers one of another after they have transgressed once for all by denying the Greek gods and by worshipping that crucified sophist himself and living under his laws. (qtd. in Tenney)[9]

Although Jesus is not named in this text, Lucian makes a clear reference to Him when he identifies Him as the lawgiver of the early movement. Lucian acknowledges the fellowship of Christian believers and their steadfast denial of Greek gods.

Early nonchristian historians testify that Jesus lived and that He was strangely more than a man. Modern nonchristian historians have had similar things to say about Christ. Will Durant was a noted modern historian. He professed no form of Christianity. His impartial estimation of Christ is as follows:

> That a few simple men should in one generation have invented so powerful and appealing a personality, so lofty an ethic and so inspiring a vision of human brotherhood, would be a miracle far more incredible than any recorded in the Gospels. After two centuries of Higher Criticism the outlines of the life, character, and teaching of Christ, remain reasonably clear, and constitute the most fascinating feature in the history of Western man.[10]

Durant's admission is no less than remarkable. He was know-
ledgeable of the contents of the New Testament and its claims for
Jesus Christ. He admits, however, that the deliberate fabrication of
the appealing personality of Christ by the disciples would have been
a miracle greater than any recorded in the New Testament. He could
not have given a greater testimonial to the Divinity of the Jesus of
history! Durant's admission lends credibility to the Josephus
quotation cited earlier which is dismissed by many scholars because
he does not sound like an unbeliever. Good historians strive to
eliminate personal bias from their records of history.

We are certainly justified in using historical testimony, but we must
understand that the validity of Christian faith does not depend upon
any historian's opinion of Christ. What a historian or anyone else
says about Christ does not alter the truth about Him. Historians
can produce convincing evidence that Christ lived and that He
profoundly changed the course of human events. But history itself
cannot, with certainty, establish that Jesus is the Divine Son of God.
Ultimately, that certainty can only be established *by trusting faith
in the heart of the believer.*

Jesus' School

Rabbinical schools, such as Jesus' school of twelve initial disciples,
were not uncommon in His day. Jesus was more than a teacher,
but He was foremost a teacher. Everything He said or did was
intended to communicate to His hearers the nature of the Father.
Jesus was frequently addressed as "Rabbi" although His school was
not recognized by Jewish authorities.

A mark of the humanity of Jesus is seen in the selection of the
men for His school. Although some people have almost deified the
disciples or imparted to them some unusually pious attributes, they
were amazingly similar to us. Peter talked too much; James and John
were men of violent tempers; Philip's faith would not let him see
past the coins in the common purse. Nathanael was a cynic; Thomas
was a doubter; Simon was a zealot, possibly meaning he was a
political activist.

Matthew was a tax collector, and tax collectors were typically
despised. Although Matthew may not have participated in the

practice, tax collectors were known for extortion. They were required to send a certain amount of their collection to Rome; the remainder was clear profit. Typically they bought their office, sold their consciences, and became very wealthy. The name "Matthew" means "gift of God." Christ must have seen something good in Matthew others did not see.

After Matthew accepted discipleship, he arranged a great feast (Luke 5:27-32). Although we are not told so, we are inclined to believe that, at the feast, Matthew made an announcement to his tax collector friends that he had a new allegiance. In his Gospel, Matthew refers to himself by the despised term "publican." He never forgot what Jesus did for him. Matthew remembered and recorded these words of Jesus: "No man can serve two masters," (Matthew 6:24) and "Seek ye first his kingdom and his righteousness" (Matthew 6:33). Matthew, like all of the rest of the disciples except Judas, paid the true cost of discipleship: loss of identity with the old self and the creation of a new identity with Jesus.

Judas Iscariot had a proud name. He was likely named after either the son of Jacob, leader of the tribe of Judah, or Judas Maccabaeus, a famous Jewish national leader during the period between the Old and New Testaments. When he was first chosen, Judas had the confidence of the other eleven disciples. They let him carry the common purse. He was probably quite capable. After all, one would expect that Matthew, the tax collector, would have been the treasurer for the small school. However, Judas had an inordinate love for money and was willing to compromise principle. Jesus chose Judas for transformation, but, in Judas' case, transformation failed.

We do not see the Deity of Jesus reflected in the men He chose for His school. They were all human, just as we are. Christ even chose one who failed Him. It is not until after the resurrection that we see the Divine wisdom of Christ reflected in the men He chose to reshape the course of history. Jesus' school certifies both His humanity and His Divinity.

The Emotions of Jesus

That Jesus is a man of history is evident from the way He expressed His feelings and emotions on several occasions. Arriving at Bethany once, Jesus was met by Mary, the sister of Lazarus. When He saw Mary and the others weeping for Lazarus, who had died, He was "deeply moved in spirit" (John 11:33). This phrase suggests that He was possibly so distressed that His body trembled. John states that it was after this expression of emotion that "Jesus wept" (John 11:35). We see here not so much the Divinity of Jesus as His humanity. Most of us have stood by the casket of a loved one and grieved deeply because someone we love has died. Jesus hurt as we hurt.

Jesus showed the emotion of compassion when, upon entering the city of Nain, He met a funeral procession. Some people would have crossed over to the other side of the street and let the procession pass. Jesus, however, observed that the person who had died was the only son of a widowed mother. She had already lost her husband, and now she had lost her only son. She obviously felt an indescribable loneliness though a large crowd was with her.

When Jesus saw her, "He had compassion on her and said to her, 'do not weep'" (Luke 7:13). He then raised her son from the dead. Although Jesus was Divine, He felt compassion for this widow. We not only see the compassion of Jesus displayed in this incident, but we also see Him feeling for one of us just as any other human being compassionately feels for another.

Jesus experienced other human sensations and emotions—such as hunger, thirst, loneliness, disgust, temptation, anger, disappointment, and pleasure. That Jesus enjoyed Himself on social occasions is seen in His presence at a wedding feast in Cana of Galilee. Wedding feasts were the most joyous of Jewish social occasions. Jesus was, *in all respects*, like we are.

The pain which Jesus experienced on numerous occasions was just as real to Him as the pain that we experience. He, no doubt, frequently had to remove an irritating grain of sand from His sandal. He became exhausted from teaching the people from dawn until dark. Sleeping in a boat bouncing with the waves on the Sea of Galilee had to be difficult and discomforting.

All of those pains paled, however, as he experienced the pain of Gethsemane and Calvary. He may have gone for approximately thirty-six hours prior to His death without sleep. During that period He experienced betrayal, denial, arrest, mock trials, a scourging which men frequently did not survive, and an indescribably horrible death by Roman crucifixion. Throughout this ordeal, He did not divest Himself of His human nature. He suffered as we would have suffered had we been there instead. He was there, in fact, *in our stead*. We must understand the humanity of Jesus in order to accept His Divinity.

Conclusion

In Hebrews 2:5-18 the writer quotes David's Psalm 8 that speaks of mankind as "made a little lower than the angels." The Hebrew writer then states, "But we see Jesus, who for a little while was made lower than the angels, crowned with glory and honor because of the suffering of death, so that by the grace of God he might taste death for every one" (v. 9). By stating that both mankind, in general, and Jesus, in particular, have been made a little lower than the angels, the writer makes clear his intention to declare the humanity of Jesus. His reason for doing so is given in verses 17 and 18:

> Therefore he had to be made *like his brethren in every respect*, so that he might become a merciful and faithful high priest in the service of God, to make expiation for the sins of the people. For because he himself has suffered and been tempted, he is able to help those who are tempted.

The Hebrew writer wants us to accept the humanity of Jesus so we can know that Christ understands our hurts, feelings, and emotions and that He will intercede for us in prayer. Christ knows us intimately, not only because He created us, but also because He was *really* a man.

Jesus, wonderful Thou art,
Wholly God in every part,
Yet Thou knowest every heart,
Dwell in us today.
                    F. M. McCann

8

Is Jesus Really the Son of God?

Jesus of Nazareth is an authentic historical personality, but is He the Son of God? The historical references in Chapter 7 present Jesus as a remarkable person, but they do not establish His Deity.

The principal literary source for our information about the nature of Jesus is the New Testament, in general, and the Gospels, in particular. Skeptics would like to discount these sources as prejudiced because Christians claim they are inspired. However, whether or not we accept them as inspired, we must recognize the New Testament documents for their historical value.

In comparison with other ancient documents, the Gospels are (a) the most extensively preserved, (b) the most critically analyzed and authenticated, (c) the most widely translated, and (d) the most generally accepted. We must, therefore, treat them fairly and accept their testimony about Jesus without prejudice. The Gospels have not been shown to be inaccurate on other major historical points; why should we question what they say about Jesus?

Not only do we have the testimony of Jesus Himself, but we also have remarkably fulfilled prophecies of His birth, life, and death. Additionally, we have valuable extrabiblical testimony. Time is universally marked by the historic event of God's stepping onto the human stage in the person of Jesus of Nazareth. The life of Jesus has inspired the world's best minds in art, poetry, literature, music, and architecture. By admiration and not by force, Jesus Christ commands more followers than the greatest military leaders the world has ever known.

The Birth of Christ

Had it been the intention of a small band of fanatical Jews to perpetrate a fraud and pass their leader off as the Son of God, they would never have devised a virgin-birth scheme. In a society that was strictly regulated by morals, social customs, and prejudices, Mary had to have been a social outcast because of her pregnancy before marriage. Perhaps that is the reason she "went with haste into the hill country" to stay with Elizabeth (Luke 1:39).

It is doubtful that skeptical citizens of Nazareth ever gave up their impression that Jesus was an illegitimate child. The fact that Christianity succeeded in spite of unbelievable tales of a virgin birth is itself remarkable evidence for the Deity of Jesus. From a human point of view, rumor of a virgin birth was no way to ensure the success of a new movement.

The birth of Jesus was a miracle which defies natural scientific explanation. However, one would not expect to be able to scientifically rationalize the virgin birth any more than he would be able to rationalize the creation of the universe. Heavenly bodies acknowledged His birth by assuming an unnatural position in the Palestinian sky. An angelic host of heaven announced His arrival by saying, "Glory to God in the highest, and on earth peace among men with whom he is pleased" (Luke 2:14). All other events in the life of Christ, including His resurrection, were made possible because of the virgin birth.

At His birth, Christ was given the name "Jesus," which fixes Him as a person in history. In prophecy His name was "Emmanuel," which means "God with us" and proclaims His Deity (Matthew 1:23). The one word "Emmanuel" expresses the essence of His mission on earth; it is the summation of the Gospel message, "God has visited man." God's pursuit of man had come to this: a babe wrapped in swaddling clothes lying in a manger, the stars of heaven and the wise of the earth adoring Him in worship.

Christ's miraculous birth was foretold in prophecy. Isaiah magnificently alludes to Christ's birth and reign as King:

> For to us a child is born, to us a son is given; and the government will be upon his shoulder, and his name will be called "Wonderful Counselor, Mighty God, Everlasting Father, Prince of Peace." Isaiah 9:6, 7

Micah's prophecy is specific in that he names the city of Christ's birth, saying,

> But you, O Bethlehem. . .from you shall come forth for me one who is to be ruler in Israel, whose origin is from old, from ancient days. Micah 5:2

Micah prophesied more than 700 years before Christ was born. His prophecy is an example of a "direct prophecy" because Matthew refers almost word for word to Micah saying, "So it is written by the prophet" (Matthew 2:5). Equally amazing is the unlikely manner in which Micah's prophecy was fulfilled.

Mary, who was betrothed to Joseph and who was soon to give birth to baby Jesus, was living in Nazareth, Galilee. Nazareth was approximately 100 miles from the prophesied birth city of the Messiah. It was unlikely that Mary, an expectant mother, would travel this far by foot or by donkey, the only means of travel. However, an unsuspecting Roman emperor, Caesar Augustus, decreed that everyone should return to his home city to be taxed, which required Joseph to go to Bethlehem, his birth city. Mary elected to join Joseph, possibly so she could be near her husband when the child was born.

It is unlikely that this incredible series of events would have occurred—except that the providential hand of God had intervened to fulfill prophecy. The fulfillment of Micah's prophecy certifies the Deity of Christ.

Equally remarkable is the fact that another unsuspecting king figured into the fulfillment of still another Old Testament prophecy. Herod, upon learning of the birth of Jesus whom the wise men called the King of the Jews, determined to destroy the child. Herod was an unwitting agent of Satan who, over the next thirty-three years, unleashed all of the evils of Hell to destroy Christ's earthly work. Mary and Joseph were warned of the danger and fled to Egypt to escape Herod. The escape route was an estimated 500-mile round trip. When the danger was over, Mary, Joseph, and the child returned to Nazareth. This series of events led to the fulfillment of another prophecy:

When Israel was a child, I loved him, and out of Egypt I called my son. Hosea 11:1

Matthew, in his Gospel, applies the Hosea text to the flight of Jesus' family into Egypt and their return to Nazareth. He makes this application because Israel, the Old Testament patriarch who fled from Egyptian bondage, typifies God's true son, Christ, who fled to and returned from Egypt.

Jesus at Age Twelve

The Gospels are virtually silent regarding the events that occurred from the return to Nazareth until Jesus' twelfth year. In a way, it is unfortunate that boys and girls today cannot know what those years in Jesus' life were like. We can surmise that He went to the village school and memorized much Scripture, which He freely quoted as an adult. He learned the value of hard work. He developed sensitive feelings for the lily of the field, the sparrow, a mother hen and her chicks, the wind, and the rain. He probably delighted in the sweet taste of goat's milk and honey.

Mary and Joseph, on occasion, thought the boy was inconsiderate, as they did the time He became separated from them in Jerusalem at the Passover. Thinking the twelve-year-old boy was with the caravan, they traveled a full day's journey toward home before they discovered that He was missing. A modern parent can appreciate the fear that Mary and Joseph must have felt when they learned that He was not with the caravan.

Mary and Joseph had to travel another day to return to Jerusalem to look for Jesus. After three days, they found Him sitting among the teachers in the temple, listening and asking questions. Jewish boys became men at the age of twelve, so it appears almost certain that by this time Jesus knew His purpose on earth. His response to Mary's scolding is revealing: "How is it that you sought me? Did you not know that I must be in my Father's house?" (Luke 2:49). He understood, but Mary and Joseph did not understand. This would not be the last time Jesus would perplex them.

The Teachings of Jesus

John's claims for Jesus are that He was in the beginning with God, that He was the agent of creation, and that He was the Son of God revealed in human flesh (John 1:1-3, 14). If John's claims are true, one should expect that Jesus' teachings would perfectly address human needs.

Jesus' ministry of teaching was immediately preceded by His baptism and temptation. At His baptism, the Spirit of God visibly descended upon Him and God acknowledged, "This is my beloved Son, with whom I am well pleased" (Matthew 3:17). The period of forty days' fasting which followed His baptism was enough to bring any healthy person to physical ruin. Since He was tempted "in all points like as we," we understand that He overcame temptation by virtue of His humanity rather than His Deity. When it was all over, Satan left Him and angels came and ministered to Him (Matthew 4:11).

After His encounter with Satan, Jesus returned to Nazareth and, as was His custom, attended synagogue worship on the Sabbath (Luke 4:17-21). At the synagogue, the attendant handed Him the scroll of Isaiah. Christ unrolled it and read these words:

The Spirit of the Lord God is upon me, because the Lord has anointed me to bring good tidings to the afflicted; he has sent me to bind up the brokenhearted, to proclaim liberty to the captives, and the opening of the prison to those who are bound; to proclaim the year of the Lord's favor, and the day of vengeance of our God; to comfort all who mourn. Isaiah 61:1, 2.

After Christ had read these words, "the eyes of all in the synagogue were fixed on him." Christ said to those present, "Today this scripture has been fulfilled in your hearing" (Luke 4:21). Jesus, then, declared Himself to be the Messiah of God, whom Isaiah had predicted 700 years earlier. After Christ spoke in the synagogue that day, all of the people "wondered at the gracious words which proceeded out of His mouth; and they said, 'is not this Joseph's son?'" (Luke 4:22).

After selecting a most unlikely school of disciples, Christ began His ministry of showing people the nature of God. His fame spread quickly as He cast out demons, healed epileptics and paralytics, and opened the eyes of the blind. We would expect Him to perform such miracles if He were Divine.

Other great teachers have given us profound thoughts but none with the consistency and grace which characterized the teachings of Jesus. His claim to Deity resulted in His being asked difficult questions. He did not hesitate to talk of payment of taxes, capital punishment, human suffering, and retribution for sins in the life hereafter. Repeatedly, the Pharisees tried to trap Him in argument. As would be expected of God's Son, He astounded the lawyers and teachers with His answers.

Under the Law of Moses, duty was the basis for human conduct. In the Sermon on the Mount, Christ taught that we must go beyond duty. The Law of Moses had served its purpose well, but Christ's law of love and grace was far superior. When Jesus concluded His Sermon on the Mount, the people observed that He was a different kind of teacher. He did not teach by quoting other scribes and rabbis; He taught them as one who was His own authority (Matthew 7:29). This was because He is God's Son.

Jesus was not a typical orthodox Jew of His day. He understood that rabbinical interpretations of the Law of Moses had made a farce of God's word. When He was asked why He ate with tax collectors and sinners, His response was not what one would expect of a brilliant rabbi. His response was what one would expect of God's Son, "I came not to call the righteous, but sinners" (Matthew 9:13). Likewise, Jesus did not violate the Sabbath as He was accused of doing; He created the Sabbath. Everything about Him and His teachings was exactly what one would have expected of Deity.

A profound teaching of Christ that separates Him from human philosophers is the "Golden Rule": "So whatever you wish that men would do to you, do so to them." (Matthew 7:12). Some critics claim that this rule of human conduct actually originated with Confucius. However, what Confucius said was, "What I do not wish others to do unto me, I also wish not to do unto others." Whereas Jesus' rule is active, Confucius' rule is passive. Confucius' rule does not require that one do anything *for* others; it only requires that one do no harm to others. According to Confucius, one is not allowed to drown another person, but he is not obligated to save another person from drowning. Confucius' rule is sometimes called the

Silver Rule.

The Brass Rule is the rule by which perhaps the majority of mankind lives: "Do to others as they would do to you." This rule for living is basically selfish and encourages retaliation. The modern version of the Brass Rule is, "Don't get mad; get even."

The Iron Rule would more aptly be described as a club or weapon of hate. Nevertheless, many people live by this rule: "Do to others what you do not want them to do to you." This rule is the basis for man's inhumanity to other men. Yet many world leaders have gained positions of power by the exercise of this rule of conduct.

It is not necessary for every teaching of Jesus to be original. If Jesus is God's Son, one expects Him to use truth from every source to frame His moral and ethical teaching. It would be no reflection on Jesus' claim had Confucius or some other great teacher first stated the Golden Rule.

The Claims of Jesus

It would take either a mentally deranged person or the Son of God to make the claims that Jesus of Nazareth made. C. S. Lewis is right when he states that the historical Jesus was either lunatic or Lord.[1] Paul is right, too, in stating that Christians are, of all men, most to be pitied if Jesus is not who He claims to be (1 Corinthians 15:19). Jesus' claims, however, were not merely idle talk. He verified His claims by the things He did.

Some of the Jews whom Jesus taught once accused him of being a madman or being possessed by a demon (John 8:49). They were sure He was a demoniac when He responded to their question, "Are you greater than our father Abraham?" by saying, "Before Abraham was, I am" (John 8:58). They took up stones to throw at Him. This claim Jesus made is one of His most remarkable. It perhaps, more than anything else, secured the determination of the Jews to kill Him. At the time Jesus made this statement, Abraham had been dead approximately 2,000 years! In other words, Jesus was claiming to be timeless, but the Jews believed that only God is timeless. They correctly understood, then, that Jesus was claiming equality with God.

After Jesus' encounter with the Jews recorded in John 8, He

proceeded to demonstrate that He was not bound by time. He immediately healed a man who had been blind from birth (John 9). By this miracle, He exercised authority over time. Jesus reversed the physiological effects of years of atrophy which typically occur in the eye sockets of a person born blind who grows to adulthood. After this miracle, the Jews were determined to kill Him. However, His claims became even more bold: "I am the good shepherd" (John 10:11); "I and the Father are one" (John 10:30).

One of the most astounding claims that Jesus makes is, "I am not of this world" (John 8:23). When He claims that He is not "of this world," He says that He is from another world, a reality transcendent to our reality. If this claim is true, Christ is the only person who has ever lived who has the authority to tell men how to think, how to relate to others, and how to go about doing things. The following evidence is offered in support of this conclusion.

The Miracles of Christ

Some people stagger at the miracles of Jesus—saying they create a basis for doubt rather than faith. However, consider what we would think of Jesus had He made the lofty claims He made but had not done anything to certify His claims. One purpose for the miracles of Jesus was to demonstrate that He was who He claimed to be, the Son of God. He claimed to be from a reality beyond this temporal world. By His miracles, Jesus verified this claim as He demonstrated authority over every aspect of human existence: time, stuff, space, gravity, and death.

JESUS OVER TIME, STUFF, SPACE, GRAVITY, AND DEATH

By healing the adult man who was born blind (John 9), Jesus reversed degenerative physical effects which had occurred over the years to the optic nerve of the man He healed. It should not surprise us that He would do this. What are a mere few years to the one who is timeless?

When Jesus turned water into wine in Cana of Galilee and when He fed the thousands by the shore of Galilee (John 2, 6), He performed creation miracles. There are chemical elements in wine which are not in water. Water consists only of hydrogen and oxygen, but wine consists of additional elements such as carbon, nitrogen, and sulfur. These new chemical elements and the compounds they compose miraculously came into existence in the water pots. By Galilee's shore, thousands of people witnessed matter coming into existence in the hands of Christ. As He broke bread He *created bread*. But what are a little wine and a few loaves of bread to the one who created the universe?

An official from Capernaum approached Jesus when He came again to Cana (John 4:46-54). His son at Capernaum, about eighteen miles away, was at the point of death from a fever. Seeing the faith of the official, Jesus healed the boy without going to Capernaum. The purpose of this miracle seems to be, in part, to demonstrate that the space of a few miles is insignificant to the one through whom all of space was created.

When Jesus walked on water early one morning, He was not trying merely to impress the disciples. Neither was He wanting to deceive them by walking on rocks in shallow water as some have claimed. Rather, He was demonstrating that He was not subject to earth's gravitation (Matthew 14:22-27). Again, what is walking on water to the one who holds the universe together by the power of His word (Colossians 1:17)?

Standing at the tomb of Lazarus (John 11), Jesus spoke, and a body that had been dead for three days and was already beginning to decay came to life. Friends unwrapped Lazarus who was bound in grave clothes. Later, Jesus demonstrated ultimate power over death by His own resurrection. The original purpose of the miracles of Jesus was to create faith and to show that He was and is God's Son. That purpose has not changed.

By demonstrating authority over stuff, time, space, gravity, and death, Jesus verified the claim, "I am not of this world" (John 8:23). Natural philosophy and natural theology attempt to interpret time and space from the perspective of time and space. It is no more possible to do this than it is for a microbe to appreciate the Mona Lisa by crawling around on the face of the canvas.

We should not be surprised that natural philosophy and natural theology lead to uncertainty and despair. The Christian, however, is not left to uncertainty and despair. He can interpret reality through the eyes of Jesus, who sees reality not from the perspective of time and space, but from the perspective of eternity! This is the Christian advantage. *Christians see reality through the eyes of Christ, and this makes all the difference!*

The Death of Christ

The fulfillment of Old Testament prophecy in the death of Christ shows that He is Divine. Christ is also a true prophet. After washing the disciples' feet to demonstrate humility and servanthood, Christ used a one-thousand-year-old text written by David to predict Judas' betrayal. He said to His disciples, "He who ate my bread has lifted his heel against me" (Psalm 41:9; John 13:18). Within minutes He dipped a morsel of food and handed it to Judas who, after receiving it, immediately went out and prepared to betray Him.

Many Bible students understand Psalm 22 to apply to Christ. It is truly an amazing and accurate description of Christ's death by crucifixion. A thousand years before Christ, David wrote:

My God, my God, why hast thou forsaken me?
   O My God, I cry by day, but thou dost not
   answer; and by night, but find no rest.
All who see me mock at me,
   they make mouths at me, they wag their heads;
I am poured out like water,
   and all my bones are out of joint;
My heart is like wax,
   it is melted within my breast;
My strength is dried up like a potsherd,
   and my tongue cleaves to my jaws;
   thou dost lay me in the dust of death.
Yea, dogs are round about me;
   a company of evildoers encircle me;
   they have pierced my hands and feet—
I can count all my bones—

they stare and gloat over me;
they divide my garments among them,
and for my raiment they cast lots.
Selected from Psalm 22:1-18

When David wrote Psalm 22, the Jews did not practice capital punishment by crucifixion. They administered the death penalty by stoning. A thousand years later, Stephen was stoned when Jewish leaders took matters into their own hands (Acts 7). That the Messiah, a Jew, would die by crucifixion after being rejected by the Jews is a truly remarkable prediction come true. Christ likely speaks of the manner of His death when He says, "And I, when I am lifted up from the earth, will draw all men to myself" (John 12:32).

The prophecy about Jesus in Isaiah 53 is accurate in remarkable detail. This prophecy came into sharp focus with the death of Christ. Isaiah prophesied that the suffering Savior would have something in common with both the wicked and the rich in His death: "And they made his grave with the wicked and with a rich man in his death, although he had done no violence, and there was no deceit in his mouth" (Isaiah 53:9). This prophecy, written 700 years before Christ, was fulfilled when Jesus was crucified between two thieves. After Jesus' death, Joseph of Arimathea, a rich man, came and requested that Pilate release the body to him. Joseph placed it in his new tomb. The exacting detail with which so many Old Testament prophecies were fulfilled during the ministry and death of Jesus is no less than amazing. Jesus must be who he claims to be, God's Son.

The Resurrection of Christ

God's pursuit of man which began in Eden did not end at Calvary. Had the story ended when Christ died on the cross, man would have been left to nothing but despair. Three days after His death, however, His tomb was empty. Many attempts to rationalize the empty tomb in natural terms have failed.

One explanation that has been given for the empty tomb is that Jesus' disciples or Joseph of Arimathea stole His body. At the time of the death of Christ, His disciples were demoralized and dejected.

Peter returned to his fishing business. We can safely assume that all of the other disciples, though sad, thought that their "Messiah" was a fake (Luke 24:21). Therefore, the disciples, including Joseph of Arimathea, had no motive for stealing the body of Jesus. The guards who had slept through the night claimed that the disciples had stolen the body (Matthew 28:13), but would any court of law accept testimony from witnesses who slept through a crime?

Two other serious attempts have been made to explain the empty tomb. One explanation is that the women mistakenly went to the wrong tomb that Sunday morning. It is incredible that this idea could be seriously proposed. Less than seventy-two hours had transpired since the women had anointed the body and watched as it had been buried. The body had been lovingly placed in a new, privately owned, public tomb, not in a cemetery with thousands of lots. The women could not have forgotten where the tomb was.

We see the desperation of skeptics in their suggestion that Jesus merely fainted on the cross. No one who has seen or researched the horrors of crucifixion would make such a suggestion. Furthermore, Jesus' executioners were professionals: they were capable of recognizing death. The body of Jesus was emaciated, drained of blood, starved, and dehydrated. Yet skeptics claim that He supposedly regained consciousness, pushed away a large stone (an act that would have surely awakened the sleeping guards), overcame the guards, and presented Himself to the disciples alive!

On the day Christ died, the disciples were demoralized, ashamed, humiliated, and embarrassed; their Lord had died the death of a common criminal. Fifty days later, however, their faith was so aflame that world powers could not extinguish it. The world has not been the same since. How can we account for this remarkable transformation? It is not logical to assume that the power of human persuasion alone could have convinced 3,000 persons to confess Christ as Lord on the day of Pentecost (Acts 2). What had happened? Why was Pentecost so successful?

Historians estimate that perhaps as many as one million people typically came to Jerusalem yearly for Passover. They were there when Christ died and many of them lingered in Jerusalem for the Pentecost festival days seven weeks later. During that fifty-day period, Jerusalem was surely alive with conversation. The people had many things to talk about. The temple priest told the story about the temple curtain, as thick as a man's hand, that had suddenly split from top to bottom at three o'clock in the afternoon when Jesus of Nazareth died on Golgotha. Everyone talked about the earthquake that had shaken the earth and caused large stones to break apart. Darkness had come over the land from noon until three o'clock, and stars had shone in the middle of the day. Perhaps the most disturbing news of all was that some people in Jerusalem had seen the dead Old Testament saints appear during that time! The people were disturbed and sought a rational explanation for the things they had personally witnessed the day Jesus died.

On Pentecost, Peter offered the rational explanation that everyone was seeking. Three thousand persons immediately accepted the explanation: "God has made him both Lord and Christ, this Jesus whom you crucified" (Acts 2:36). Soon the number of believers grew to 5,000, then 15,000, and the number continued to multiply.

CHRISTIANITY IS ROOTED IN HISTORY

Christianity is indeed rooted in history, not in myth or legend. To this day, honest, intelligent men and women consider the evidence and make the rational decision to follow Christ as Lord, for indeed He is!

Conclusion

A vast body of evidence supports the biblical claim that Christ is the Son of God. Without Christ, all of reality is a giant puzzle—with the most important piece missing; it does not make sense. Christ tells us who we are, whose we are, and what we are. *Through the eyes of Christ, Christians can interpret reality from the perspective of eternity. This is the Christian advantage!*

Thy word is a lamp to my feet and a light to my path.
                              Psalm 119:105

9

Is God Silent?

Suppose for a moment that you are a person who has never heard about Christianity or, for that matter, about God, Christ, or the Bible. While wandering through the aisles of a library, you pick up a book and begin to thumb through its pages. The book looks interesting, so you begin to read it. Soon you observe that it is a book that proposes to tell you about the origin of the universe, the origin of man, and man's purpose for existing. The book also tells you about God, who created the universe, and how He has revealed His nature to humanity. It tells you how to find peace with God, and, finally, it tells you about the destiny of the human race.

Most likely, your reaction to such a book would be one of suspicion. That is how many people respond to the Bible. The fact that the Bible proposes authoritative answers to life's greatest questions has made it the most intriguing text ever composed. The Bible has universal appeal as attested by the fact that the entire Bible has been translated into approximately 250 languages.

Although written records are known that predate the Bible, the oldest book of the Bible was composed about 3500 years ago. The last book of the Bible, Revelation, was written 1600 years later. The Bible was originally written in Hebrew, Aramaic, and Greek. Its approximately forty authors were scattered over three continents. They came from a wide variety of backgrounds. Among the writers of the Bible, we find a king, a physician, shepherds, judges, and fishermen. Yet their writings show an astounding consistency as they follow one theme: God's pursuit of fallen man.

Other books such as the Book of Mormon, the Koran of Islam, the Veda of the Hindu religion, and the Tripitaka of Buddhism, make claims of having their origin in deity. God, in the Bible, has always

93

invited the discriminating person to compare His words with the words of other "prophets": "How long will you go limping with two different opinions? If the Lord is God, follow him; but if Baal, then follow him" (1 Kings 18:21). Although there are other books which people hold to be sacred, the Bible claims God-breathed uniqueness that sets it apart from other religious literature.

Concepts of Inspiration

When we say that the Bible claims uniqueness, we are saying that the Bible claims to be completely unlike any other book. Other books may claim to have their origin in deity, but the Bible is distinctly different. Some believe that the Bible is *naturally inspired*, that is, it is like books man has written in terms of origin. However, the Bible is set apart from great works of literature (such as the works of Shakespeare, Burns, or Keats) which are "inspired" by mood or human intelligence.

Other people believe that the Bible was *dictated* by the Holy Spirit to man. However, there is considerable evidence that the human authors of the Bible were not merely passive instruments or secretaries through whom the Holy Spirit produced the Bible. Still other persons believe that the writers of the Bible were only *partially inspired* in that the Holy Spirit gave them an idea or general plot. They were then inspired merely by mood and human intelligence. This is not the biblical concept of inspiration, either. What, then, does the Bible teach about its inspiration?

The Biblical Claim to Inspiration

Evans points out in H.C. Theissen's *Introduction to the New Testament* that the biblical writers claim that God spoke through them as many as 3,800 times.[1] Frequently, they use such expressions as "Thus says the Lord" or "The Lord spoke to me saying." Old Testament prophets are not ambiguous in their claim to being spokesmen for God. Israel's King David says, "The Spirit of the Lord speaks by me, his word is upon my tongue" (2 Samuel 23:2). Jeremiah, who repeatedly warned against false prophets, writes,

94

"Then the Lord put forth his hand and touched my mouth; and the Lord said to me 'Behold, I have put my words in your mouth.'" (Jeremiah 1:9).

After assembling His school of twelve disciples, Christ sent them out to preach the message, "The kingdom of heaven is at hand." Anticipating that they would be rejected and possibly persecuted, Jesus assured them that, in their hour of personal defense, they were not to be anxious about what they should say. He told them, "For it is not you who speak, but the Spirit of your Father speaking through you" (Matthew 10:20). Later, knowing that He would soon leave them, Jesus told the disciples, "The Counselor, the Holy Spirit, whom the Father will send in my name, he will teach you all things, and bring to your remembrance all that I have said to you" (John 14:26). We may safely assume that this promise applies to what the disciples wrote as well as to what they spoke.

Jewish synagogues of Jesus' and Paul's day contained scrolls of sacred writings which were read aloud in public synagogue services. These scrolls were among the most highly treasured possessions of the Jewish community. They contained only Old Testament documents inasmuch as the New Testament had not yet been written. Paul's missionary method typically was to enter Jewish synagogues and reason from the scrolls of the sacred writings that Jesus was the Christ (Acts 17:2).

The Apostle Paul is referring to the Old Testament sacred writings when he writes to Timothy:

> From childhood you have been acquainted with the sacred writings which are able to instruct you for salvation through faith in Christ Jesus. All scripture is inspired by God and profitable for teaching, for reproof, for correction, and for training in righteousness, that the man of God may be complete, equipped for every good work.
> 2 Timothy 3:15-17

Timothy had been reared by a Jewish mother. Apparently she had carefully taught him the sacred writings. Paul's claim is that those writings were inspired and adequate to make one spiritually complete in Christ. Paul's use of the word "inspired," *theopneustos*, is found only here in the New Testament and carries the meaning of "God-breathed." Paul clearly states that Scripture is inspired or God-breathed, but he says nothing of how God worked to inspire

Scripture.

Paul wanted the Galatian Christians to understand that he did not receive his knowledge of God's message "second-hand" from anyone. In particular, he did not receive his knowledge from the Jerusalem apostles, and neither was he inferior to the Jewish false teachers who followed him preaching their doctrine of works, which opposed his doctrine of grace. To the Galatians, Paul states:

> For I would have you know, brethren, that the gospel which was preached by me is not man's gospel. For I did not receive it from man, nor was I taught it, but it came through a revelation of Jesus Christ. Galatians 1:11, 12

Paul's proof of such an imposing claim was his own conversion to Christianity (Galatians 1:13-24). To be sure, the conversion of Saul of Tarsus is one of the great testimonies to the historical authenticity of the Christian religion (Acts 9, 22).

The Corinthian Christians were special to Paul. That anyone could be spiritual in the wicked city of Corinth was itself a testimony to the power of the Gospel. It was a city where men worshiped human wisdom and human deities. In the following selections, Paul acknowledges God as the source of his wisdom:

> My speech and my message were not in plausible words of [human] wisdom, but in demonstration of the Spirit and of power. . .we impart a secret and hidden wisdom of God, which God decreed before the ages. For the Spirit searches everything, even the depths of God. No one comprehends the thoughts of God except the Spirit of God. Now we received not the spirit of the world, but the Spirit which is from God, that we might understand the gifts bestowed on us by God. And we impart this in words not taught by human wisdom but taught by the Spirit, interpreting spiritual truths to those who possess the Spirit. Selected from 1 Cor. 2:4-13

Messianic prophecies in the sacred writings of the Old Testament were shrouded in mystery until Christ came. Then they were brought sharply into focus. We see Messianic prophecies much more clearly today. Peter acknowledges this fact in two selections from his writings which contribute significantly to our understanding of biblical inspiration.

In the first selection, Peter states that Messianic prophets, such as Jeremiah, Isaiah, and David, did not have a clear focus on the meaning of their own prophecies. After they wrote, they searched for the meaning of what they had written:

> The prophets who prophesied of the grace that was to be yours searched and inquired about this salvation; they inquired what person or time was indicated by the Spirit of Christ within them when predicting the sufferings of Christ and the subsequent glory. 1 Peter 1: 10, 11

It is of interest that, on occasion, the apostles did not fully understand things they proclaimed. For example, on Pentecost, Peter said that the promise of God was "to all who are afar off" thus including the Gentiles (Acts 2:39). Later, at Joppa, Peter was given a vision by which God showed him that God is no respecter of persons. At the house of Cornelius, the first Gentile convert, the meaning of the vision first became clear to Peter: God had included the Gentiles (Acts 10:28). It is, therefore, apparent that, in the Pentecost sermon, Peter had not been fully aware of the meaning of his own message!

In a second selection from Peter's writings, Peter underscores the extreme importance of what he is about to say with the introduction, *"First of all you must understand this"*:

> First of all you must understand this, that no prophecy of scripture is a matter of one's own interpretation, because no prophecy ever came by the impulse of man, but men moved by the Holy Spirit spoke from God. 2 Peter 1:20, 21

What Peter said was indeed very important. However, this text has frequently been misunderstood. Some have concluded that individuals are not to interpret Scripture. Rather, they say, Scripture is to be interpreted by the Church, priests, or some authority *for* the people. This is not the intention of this text at all. Every reader of Scripture should not only interpret the meaning of Scripture without bias; he should also translate it into personal, obedient faith. This is a high and exalted privilege for every reader of Scripture.

When Peter states that "prophecy of Scripture is not a matter of one's own interpretation" he speaks of the *writing* of Scripture and not the *reading* of Scripture. He says that prophecy of Scripture did not have its origin in the mind of the prophet; it had its origin with

God. Furthermore, the prophets were moved or "borne along," not by the impulse of man, but by the impulse or will of the Holy Spirit. False prophets spoke their own ideas (Jeremiah 23:16, Ezekiel 13:2, 3), but true prophets spoke from God. Peter's claim is that Scripture originated with God.

The Human Character of the Bible

When Christ was on earth He was God's Word in human flesh. It is necessary to understand Christ's human nature in order to have a trusting faith in His Divine nature. The Bible is also God's Word. Understanding its human character helps us to have a trusting faith in its Divine character.

The Holy Spirit mediated God's written word to man *through* man. The Biblical writers were vessels of clay just as much as you and I are. David, who gave us many of the Psalms, lusted for Bathsheba and had Uriah, her husband, slain. However, he repented of his sins and wrote the beautiful 51st Psalm. Jonah ran from God's presence; Peter denied that he even knew Christ; Paul admitted having to buffet his body constantly to keep it under subjection to the Spirit of Christ. No biblical writer is portrayed as anything more than human. Yet, without exception, each one directs the Bible reader's thoughts to Christ.

Human biblical writers used human literary techniques in communicating God's message. *The Bible is not only an inspired book; it is a book of inspired literature.* As the writers were carried along by the Holy Spirit, they used a variety of literary techniques: prose, poetry, parallelism, simile, allegory, metaphor, hyperbole, irony, proverbs, and history. Jeremiah's style is different from Isaiah's, and Luke does not write like Paul. In the Gospels, Matthew assumes primarily a Jewish reading audience, Mark assumes a Roman audience, and Luke, a Greek audience. John uses a rather limited vocabulary and a simple writing style but communicates lofty spiritual concepts.

Since the biblical writers use different literary styles, one does not expect the Bible to be uniformly easy to understand. In fact, the opposite is true. Peter, although inspired himself, admits that parts of Paul's inspired letters are difficult to understand:

So also our beloved brother Paul wrote to you according to the wisdom given him, speaking of this as he does in all his letters. There are some things in them hard to understand, which the ignorant and unstable twist to their own destruction, as they do the other scriptures. 2 Peter 3:15, 16

It would be interesting to know which of Paul's writings Peter was thinking about when he wrote this. Peter likely found the same texts difficult which we do. Even though he found some of Paul's writings difficult, he still classified them among the *other sacred writings* of the synagogue scrolls (2 Peter 3:15, 16). Peter could not have held Paul's letters in higher esteem than that.

Message Is More Important Than Words

It is apparent that, in the writing of Scripture, words were carefully chosen. One can easily imagine Paul pacing back and forth groping for words as he dictated Romans to Tertius (Romans 16:22). The weight of the evidence causes us to conclude that *words of the original text were inspired by the Holy Spirit*. For example, Jeremiah says, "the Lord said to me, behold, I have put my words in your mouth" (Jeremiah 1:9). Both Christ and Paul argued on the precise use of a single word which they quoted from Scripture (John 10:34, Galatians 3:16). However, more important than words, *per se*, is the *intended message conveyed by those words*.

For example, Christ states,

For truly I say to you, if you have faith as a grain of mustard seed, you will say to this mountain, "Move from here to there," and it will move; and nothing will be impossible to you. Matthew 17:20

What did Christ intend by this statement? Some have concluded that since they cannot literally move mountains, or even a little hill, they do not have enough faith to please God. This is a good illustration of the fact that although *words are inspired*, the intended message is more important than words. Christ is speaking in hyperbole; He does not say that we should literally expect to move mountains with faith. Rather He says, "Even if you have just a little faith, God can do great things through you."

Likewise when David writes, "The Lord is my shepherd" (Psalm 23:1), he does not mean that God is a literal shepherd and we are literal sheep. Rather he means, "God takes care of me as a shepherd takes care of his sheep." Christ did not intend for us to take literally the words, "This is my body" (Mark 14:22) during our observance of the Lord's Supper. Most passages in the Bible must be understood literally. However, in reading the Bible, we should be constantly alert to the intended message of the writer.

Christ's Attitude Toward Scripture

Perceptive readers of this chapter probably will have already noticed that I have not suggested a theory or concept of *how* inspiration occurred. That is because Scripture is silent on this subject. Far more important than adopting a theory of inspiration is identifying and emulating Christ's attitude toward Scripture. If we seriously regard Christ as *Lord*, the *Word* of God, and the agent of creation, then His attitude toward Scripture will become our attitude. Paul commands us to have the mind of Christ (Philippians 2:5). Surely that includes our adopting His view of Scripture.

As a child, Christ was carefully taught the Scriptures. His parents were dedicated believers and annually walked almost 100 miles to Jerusalem to observe the Passover (Luke 2:41). As a young man, Christ developed the habit of regular synagogue worship (Luke 4:16). He memorized much Scripture which He quoted as an adult to resist the temptations of Satan. Among His last words on the cross were, "Father, into thy hands I commit my spirit" (Luke 23:46; Psalm 31:5). William Barclay states, "He died with the child's good-night prayer on his lips".[2] Evidently, Psalm 31:5 was a "Now-I-lay-me-down-to-sleep" bedtime prayer which Jewish mothers taught their children.

Although Christ's law of love transcended the Mosaic law of works, Christ never spoke lightly of the Law of Moses. On one occasion, He was forced to make a decision between the strictness of the Law of Moses and His law of love and compassion. On that occasion, He refused to oppose the Law of Moses and authorized stoning a guilty adulterous woman to death as prescribed by the Law, but He stipulated, "Let him who is without sin among you be the first to throw a stone at her" (John 8:7).

Christ frequently expressed confidence in the truth of Old Testament events such as the creation of man and woman (Mark 10:2-6), the changing of Lot's wife into a pillar of salt (Luke 17:26-32), and the meeting of Jonah and the large fish (Matthew 12:40). Christ, the Word of God, the agent of creation, regarded these stories as authentic. He regarded Scripture as fully God-breathed. We who call Him "Lord" should think no less of God's Word.

Christ Should Be the Focus of Faith

Certain tragedy awaits a person who focuses *on the windshield* of his car as he drives down the road. Rather, one must *look through* the windshield to the road ahead. Using this analogy, *Scripture is a lens through which we see Christ*. Christ, not the Bible, is the focus of the Christian's faith. In Jesus' day, many people made the mistake of focusing on the scrolls in the synagogues; they did not use the sacred writings to see the Christ of prophecy. Jesus explained to them that this was a tragic mistake:

> You do not have his word abiding in you, for you do not believe him whom he has sent. You search the scriptures, because you think that in them you have eternal life; and it is they that bear witness to me; yet you refuse to come to me that you may have life. John 5:38, 39

The people to whom Jesus spoke these words had a misplaced faith. Their faith was in the scrolls and the physical searching of the sacred writings, not in learning the message of Scripture. They attached to their bodies leather pouches on which were written favorite Old Testament Scriptures. Jesus' point was that such activity does not guarantee holiness. God's Word must be written upon the heart and translated into obedience.

Conclusion

God is not silent; He has spoken to us in His Word, the Bible. It would be a tragic mistake, however, if one's attention were inordinately drawn to the physical book we call the Bible rather than to the Christ of the Bible. Although we believe the Bible to be a Divine product and God's Word, the focus of our faith must be on the Christ we read about in the Bible. He is the treasure of treasures; He is the pearl of great price.

O how love I thy law!
It is my meditation all the day.
                Psalm 119:97

10

Is the Bible God's Word?

God desires that Christians walk by faith and not by sight. The human tendency is to reverse the biblical priority. One walks by sight when the eye of his mind focuses on evidence rather than on Christ. Evidence should never become the object of faith, for that would be fatal to faith. I do not intend for the following evidence that the Bible is inspired to exclude faith; rather it should show that belief in the Bible makes sense.

What Constitutes Acceptable Evidence?

The first criterion for acceptable evidence is that it must be honest and factual. The Christian must not falsify data to strengthen his case. Paul says, "We have renounced disgraceful, underhanded ways; we refuse to practice cunning or to tamper with God's word" (2 Corinthians 4:2). Likewise, we should not falsify or fabricate any evidence to support the Christian position.

Christian faith is not a sinking ship. Christians do not need to grab at straws. Those who resort to such tactics either do not understand the nature of faith, or they do not understand the basis for faith. Christian faith is not only *not inferior*; it is *superior* to all faith alternatives. The Apostle Paul proudly stood on Mars Hill in the presence of the most intelligent people of his day and proclaimed the Christian message (Acts 17). He was never apologetic for his faith, and neither should we be.

A second criterion for acceptable evidence is that it must have some convincing power. This does not mean that the *fact* of inspiration depends upon the quality of the evidence. The Bible is either a God-breathed book or it is not. What has been done regarding the formation of the Bible has been done. Nothing we can say or do for or against the Bible will change that. Weak evidence is no reflection on the Bible; it is a reflection on the evidence or on the one who presents the evidence.

The Content of Scripture

Evidence supporting the uniqueness of the Bible is typically classified as either internal or external to Scripture. External evidence, such as that from archaeology or science, generates more excitement and interest. However, the greatest weight of evidence for biblical uniqueness is not found in science and archaeology. It is found in the message of Scripture itself.

The message of Scripture is sublime. The biblical plot runs like a continuous crimson thread from the fall of Adam and Eve in Eden to Calvary. Each of the approximately forty biblical writers wove the thread into the fabric of human redemption. The fabric became God's gift of grace to humanity through Jesus Christ, His son, at Calvary.

The Bible is not only a guide which God has given to man to direct him from earth to Heaven; it is also a book telling him how to live. The Bible tells men and women how to create marriages pleasing to God, rear their children, live obediently under civil authority, and perform responsibly at places of work. Paul's message to the Galatian Christians is that freedom is found in doing what is right (Galatians 5).

Although the Bible is not a psychology textbook any more than it is a science or mathematics textbook, it contains valuable principles to help us live with ourselves and our fellow man. Scripture teaches that mankind is created not on the level of the animals, but a little lower than the angels. Therefore, he has dignity and worth. One may believe, if he wishes, that he is created in the image of brute beasts, but God's Word says he is created in the image of God.

The moral standards of the Bible are unparalleled among the religious books of the world. A society that does not recognize the moral imperatives which are found in the Ten Commandments cannot hope to stand for long.

In contrast to the Bible, the Koran sanctions Islamic "holy wars" which, at one time, spread at a phenomenal rate with the aid of fire and sword. Buddhist writings were composed 400 years after the death of Buddha and have their basis in sorrow and suffering. They offer only hope of an annihilation of feeling, called Nirvana, at death. One achieves Nirvana not by accepting a doctrine of grace and forgiveness but by saving oneself by right beliefs, feelings, speech, efforts, and meditation.

The high moral standards of the Bible are often attacked by those who observe that God ordered the Israelites to utterly destroy the Canaanites (Numbers 21:3). Upon closer examination, however, one actually sees that the mercy of the Lord was extended to the Canaanites. Approximately 650 years before Israel entered Canaan, God promised Abraham that his descendants would occupy the land. God explained to Abraham that the reason why he and his family did not go immediately into Canaan was that "the iniquity of the Amorites was not yet complete" (Genesis 15:16). God gave the Canaanites an extension of grace, but they grew more and more corrupt.

The Biblical Doctrine of Christ

What Scripture says about Jesus Christ is the supreme evidence that the Bible is of Divine, not human, origin. If no other evidence existed except the biblical portrayal of Christ, one would still be constrained to acknowledge that the Bible has its origin in God, not man. The nature and mission of Christ transcend all human intellect. No person or group of persons could have contrived and executed the idea of the Christ of Scripture.

The anticipation of Christ is introduced in Genesis 3:15, when God pronounced a curse upon the serpent, saying,

I will put enmity between you and the woman,
and between your seed and her seed;
He shall bruise your head,
and you shall bruise his heel.

105

Thus begins the focus of Scripture on Christ. Beginning with Genesis 3:15 Scripture looks forward to the Christ of Calvary. From Calvary to the book of Revelation, it looks back to Calvary.

Christ is the answer to the longing of every human heart. Truth that is found only in Christ is what is needed by every natural philosopher and natural theologian. Reality makes sense only when seen through the perspective of His eyes. Without Him, the human condition is a mystery that cannot be explained, a puzzle that cannot be solved, a riddle that cannot be answered.

The Biblical Concept of God

Skeptics claim that the God of the Bible is an anthropomorphic God because Bible writers describe Him in human terms having such features as eyes, a heart, and hands. The skeptics claim that, throughout ancient times, the idea of God evolved in the mind of man and that God, therefore, is a figment of man's imagination.

It is true that God is described in anthropomorphic terms in the Bible, but that does not mean that the idea of God originated with man. The God revealed in the Bible is distinctly different from concepts of gods which man has devised. The gods conceived by man are typically like man, but the God of the Bible is completely above and beyond man.

For example, approximately 500 years before Moses led the Israelites out of Egypt, ancient Babylonians and Sumerians worshiped their gods. The Babylonian account of creation is preserved in a document called the *Enuma elish* ("When above"). In this creation account, the Babylonian gods were co-eternal with matter whereas, in the biblical account of creation, God created all things.

According to the Babylonian legend, a bloody war developed among the gods. Marduk, the "wisest of the gods," split the skull of the goddess Tiamat, cut her arteries, caused the North Wind to carry her blood southward to out-of-the-way places, and finally divided her body into two parts—with which he created the universe. Compare this account with the simple and profound biblical statement, "In the beginning God created the heavens and the earth" (Genesis 1:1).

106

A few years ago, archaeologists were exploring the remains of Chan Chan, Peru. They came upon a small room containing the remains of adolescent girls. The meaning of this discovery was unclear until they found evidence that in that room 500 years ago, Peruvian Indians had appeased their concept of the gods by human sacrifice.[1] Their concept of deity was a human concept; they thought that God was like man and desired human sacrifice. The God who reveals Himself in the Bible forbids human sacrifice (Leviticus 18:21; 20:1-5).

Also, about 500 years ago, Inca Indians sacrificed young boys to the sun god by taking them to the tops of mountains 20,000 feet high, stripping them of protective clothing, and placing them in mountain top repositories where they instantly froze to death.[2] Chill factors reached 100 degrees below zero and wind speeds reached 125 miles per hour. The Inca's concept of deity was also a human concept and unlike that of the God who reveals Himself in Scripture.

A graphic portrayal of the difference between the human concept of a deity, Baal, and the transcendent God of the Bible is found in 1 Kings 18. Elijah challenged the Israelites to make up their minds to follow either Baal or Jehovah. A contest was planned to see whether Baal or Jehovah would consume a sacrificial offering. The prophets of Baal danced around the altar from morning until noon and cried out, "O Baal, answer us" (I Kings 18:26).

In the afternoon, they continued their ritual and cut themselves with swords and lances until the blood gushed out upon them. They raved until the evening, but Baal did not respond because *Baal had been created in their image.* In contrast, Elijah's God sent fire to consume the offering when Elijah entreated Him. This God who reveals Himself in the Bible was not made in man's image; man *was created in God's image.*

God's Names

The name of the Phoenician and Moabite idol god, Baal, means "master or lord." Other pagan gods had such names as "Marduk" and "Dagon," or they were named after the planets, such as Mercury, Jupiter, and Venus. Collectively, the names for the God of the Bible are an indication of the uniqueness of Scripture. This is because man did not name God; God named Himself.

For example, the God who reveals Himself to us in the Bible is "El," which means the "strong and mighty one, the powerful one." "Elohim" is the plural form of the name and is used in Genesis 1, possibly suggesting the presence of God the Father, Christ the Son, and the Holy Spirit at creation. "El" was also the general name that was used for God in ancient Semitic languages. God uses "El" with other names to further reveal His nature to mankind. For example, some scholars claim "El-Shaddai" means "the omnipotent (all powerful) one" (Genesis 17:1).

God named Himself when He appeared to Moses at the burning bush declaring, "I AM WHO I AM" (Exodus 3:14). When Moses asked God who he should say sent him to deliver Israel, God responded, "Tell them I AM has sent you." The word "Yahweh" or "JHVH" became a basis for God to reveal His nature to man. The word "Jehovah" is not a name for God; it is a mixture of the vowels of the Hebrew word for Lord (Adonay) and the consonants JHVH, a word Jews held sacred and avoided pronouncing.

Jehovah assured Gideon that He would deliver Israel from the Midianites. Gideon, miraculously convinced that God would keep His promise, built an altar at Ophrah and called it "Jehovah-Shalom" which means "The Lord is peace" (Judges 6:24).

Ezekiel prophetically anticipates the heavenly kingdom and proclaims "Jehovah-Shammah" which means, "The Lord is there" (Ezekiel 48:35). Ezekiel, therefore, declares that Jehovah is the one and the only one who exists eternally, from everlasting to everlasting.

Abraham named the place where God spared Isaac on Mt. Moriah "Jehovah-Jireh" meaning "The Lord will provide" (Genesis 22:14). God's providential care over those who obey Him is one of the central doctrines of the Bible. In all of these names, God reveals Himself and His nature to man.

God's nature is not completely revealed in any one of the names He uses for Himself in the Old Testament. However, the complete and perfect revelation of the nature of God was in the *logos*, the Word that became flesh, Jesus Christ, who was seen, touched, and heard by man (John 1:1, 14; 1 John 1:1). Collectively, all of these names for God, including the *logos*, are words by which God reveals His nature to man. What they tell us about God constitutes strong evidence that the Bible is Divinely inspired.

The Calmness With Which Biblical Writers Wrote

Another example from within the Bible that shows that its composition was guided by the Holy Spirit is the calm writing style which characterizes Scripture. Uninspired writers are inclined to punctuate their writings with adjectives such as "amazing," "stupendous," and "colossal." However, biblical writers address such themes as the creation of the universe, the virgin birth of Christ, and His death and resurrection with a remarkable calmness. One would expect God to exercise such calmness, but not men who write by human impulse alone.

It is natural for writers to want to claim originality for the things they write. Books and journals are copyrighted; very little literature is written anonymously. Yet contrary to human nature, the biblical writers attribute authorship of their ideas to God. They write to honor God and Christ—not themselves. Over 100 times Jeremiah attributes authorship of his text to Jehovah. Approximately twenty-eight times Malachi repeats this claim in his short book. The fact that the authors voluntarily divested themselves of credit for the things they wrote supports the biblical claim to inspiration.

The way common men from ordinary walks of life addressed lofty themes in the Bible also indicates uniqueness. In Acts 4:13 we are told that Peter and John were described by those who opposed them as common, uneducated men. This was a true statement, and it would properly describe many other biblical writers also. Yet they wrote of lofty, and often transcendent, themes in such a way that they have amazed many of the great scholars of the world. Only by Divine inspiration could John, an uneducated fisherman of his day, have written the Gospel which bears his name.

Not all the Bible writers were uneducated. The Apostle Paul was highly educated, having received his training under the scholarly Gamaliel. Paul later taught in the school of Tyrannus. Yet concerning the things he wrote and spoke, he says, "For I did not receive it from man, nor was I taught it, but it came through a revelation of Jesus Christ" (Galatians 1:12). The book of Romans and the letter to the Ephesians especially bear marks of transcendence of human intellect and inspiration.

The Impartiality of the Bible

Among the great heroes of the Bible are Adam and Eve, the first man and woman; Abraham, the father of the Israelite nation; Sarah, Abraham's wife; David, King of Israel; the apostles; and, of course, Christ. Uninspired writers would be expected to gloss over the errors of their heroes. Except for Christ, all biblical characters are portrayed as mere men and women with human tendencies.

For example, Abraham twice lied about his relationship to his wife, Sarah, saying she was his sister. (She was actually his half-sister). In Egypt, his lie resulted in plagues on Pharaoh's house. Yet, in spite of this failure on the part of Abraham, God made him the father of all the faithful.

David's reign as king of Israel typified Christ's reign over spiritual Israel, the church. David is a key person in the lineage connecting Adam, Abraham, and Christ. Yet the story of David's adulterous relationship with Bathsheba and his plot to have Uriah, her husband, slain tarnishes forever the record of Israel's greatest king.

We have already seen that each of the twelve disciples which Christ chose to change the course of history were fully human. No effort was made to portray them as anything more than vessels of clay through whom God worked to effect His purposes. Paul says that God's power is perfected in human weakness (2 Corinthians 12:9).

The Beauty and Simplicity of Christian Worship

The emphasis that men have placed on the externals of Christian worship the last 2,000 years are an indication of how uninspired men might have written the Bible. Ornate but unoccupied cathedrals are beautiful monuments to Christian influence in architecture. Cathedrals and elaborate worship services conducted within their walls, however, do no justice to the simple Christian worship we read about in the New Testament.

Early Christian worship assemblies were apparently conducted in homes (Romans 16:5, 1 Corinthians 16:19, Philippians 2). Worship consisted of reading the sacred writings, preaching, teaching, *a cappella* singing, and observing the Lord's Supper. Even during persecution, the early Christians met among the catacombs and in other secret places. They took refuge—not in ornate buildings and elaborate services—but in the promise of Jesus, "For where two or three are gathered in my name, there am I in the midst of them" (Matthew 18:20).

God accepts the worship of Christian prisoners and refugees. Sometimes they have silently worshiped from prison cells or tapped secret messages to fellow prisoners through plumbing. God delights in the heart of one who is right with Him.

The simplicity of the Lord's Supper as a memorial to Christ is not the kind of memorial man would have devised. A memorial like Mt. Rushmore is typical of the way man thinks. A memorial of unleavened bread and the juice of the grape are the way God thinks. God has always been more interested in internals than in externals (1 Samuel 16:7).

The Influence of the Bible

Most of the world's best paintings, architecture, sculpture, and music have been inspired by biblical themes. Wherever the Bible has been taken and its principles applied, it has lifted human nature to a nobler plane. The Bible condemns interracial prejudice, although professing Christians have been slow to recognize the fact. The status of womanhood is highest where the Bible has had an influence.

Scientific research has progressed in societies where biblical influence has first penetrated. The reason is apparent: one would not expect man to pursue scientific research in pantheistic societies in which man worships nature. If God resides in the rocks, one would not perform a chemical analysis on rocks. If God resides in the insects and rodents, one would not be interested in discovering an insecticide or rodenticide. Jainism, a form of Hinduism, forbids men to till the soil for fear of harming insects. Well-fed rats dwell in temples while humans go hungry. Such conditions contribute to the spread of disease as well as famine.

Try to imagine what the world would be like if it were suddenly stripped of all Judaeo-Christian influences. Most of the world's best art, literature, music, and science would disappear.

111

Preservation of the Bible

It is a challenge to some people's faith that we do not have any of the original autographs of the documents of the Bible. Nevertheless we do have either hand copies or copies *of* copies of the original autographs. The John Rylands fragment of the Gospel of John, dated to the first half of the second century, is our oldest fragment of the New Testament. In view of the human tendency to worship artifacts, it is probably in the best interest of faith that we do not have the authentic autographs.

Today we have, in whole or in part, approximately 5,400 New Testament Greek manuscripts and 2,475 Latin manuscripts.[3] Furthermore, it is estimated that most of the New Testament could be reconstructed from the quotations used by the Apostolic Fathers who wrote during the period A.D. 90 to 150. In contrast, we have only about fifty manuscripts of the plays of Aeschylus, 100 manuscripts of Sophocles, and nine or ten good manuscripts of Caesar's Gallic Wars. The remarkable preservation of the Bible is a testimony to the truthfulness of Jesus' claim, "Heaven and earth will pass away, but my words will not pass away" (Mark 13:31).

Efforts to Destroy the Bible

According to tradition, each of the disciples died a martyr's death. Also, according to tradition, Peter requested to be crucified head downward because he felt he was not worthy to die as his Lord died. These traditions cannot be validated by historical testimony. However, we can validate that the blood of Christian martyrs has flowed for nearly 2,000 years as men and women have died rather than renounce their Lord. Among the last words of the elder Polycarp (A.D. 70-156) were these: "Fourscore and six years have I been his servant and he hath done me no wrong. How then can I blaspheme my King who saved me?"[4]

Throughout history, there have been repeated concerted efforts to destroy the Bible or curtail its influence. During the reigns of Roman emperors Decius (249-251) and Diocletian (284-305), personal possession of the Scriptures was a capital offense. Christians were put into dungeons, beheaded, burned at the stake, and mutilated by beasts. Extreme persecution such as this did not, however, curtail the influence of the Bible.

During the medieval period, few copies of the Bible existed because copies were handmade. Bibles were expensive. They were, therefore, chained to pulpits to keep people from stealing them. Religious authorities in the medieval church discouraged people from reading the Bible. They thought that the masses were incapable of properly interpreting the Bible without assistance. The position of Scripture, however, is that every man or woman is free to study and understand Scripture, independent of human authority.

Another effort to eliminate the Bible came as the result of attempts of skeptics like Voltaire, Paine, and Ingersoll during the 18th and 19th centuries. Voltaire boasted that he would personally destroy the Bible. However, twenty-five years after his death, the Geneva Bible Society purchased his home and converted it into a storehouse for the distribution of Bibles.

No other literary work has been as critically evaluated and extensively scrutinized as the Bible. Will Durant, a noted historian of the 20th century, did not accept the Bible as inspired. He observed, however, that if other literary sources were as critically evaluated as the Bible, they would fade into legend. He said,

> In the enthusiasm of its discoveries the higher criticism has applied to the New Testament tests of authenticity so severe that by them a hundred ancient worthies—e.g., Hammurabi, David, Socrates— would fade into legend.[5]

Conclusion

Christians must not take intellectual pleasure in merely studying the evidences for the inspiration of the Bible. Faith does not have its basis in the satisfaction that the Christian argument is a sound argument. The Bible is God's Word and must be instilled within the heart, written upon the mind, and translated into human conduct. May God bless us with the faith of our fathers, a faith by which to live and die.

How shall the young secure their hearts,
And guard their lives from sin?
Thy word the choicest rules impart
to keep the conscience clean.

Isaac Watts

11

Can I Trust My Bible?

I have before me a small book in which the author claims there are 4,000 errors and contradictions in the Bible. Books that are critical of the Bible are occasionally published. It is not my purpose here to answer all the critics. I cannot, however, ignore that the author of the book in front of me has not fairly represented Scripture. Throughout the book, he has taken passages out of context and misrepresented the Bible. It is unfortunate that most critics do not give the Bible the same courtesy and fair treatment they give other historical documents.

It is serious, indeed, if Scripture can be shown to contain inaccuracies. In Chapter 10 we presented evidence to support the claim that the Bible is God's Word. In this chapter we will examine evidence supporting the viewpoint that God has spoken *accurately*.

The Christian should expect the Bible to be accurate. If God is all-powerful and all-wise, one would expect Him to speak accurately. Nature, which God created, is carefully regulated by laws which are dependable; nature is never self-contradictory. The Christian should expect God's revealed word, the Bible, to be just as dependable as nature because both are revelations from God.

How Is the Accuracy of the Bible Tested?

When one speaks of the *accuracy* of the Bible, he refers to the truthfulness of the Bible. For example, Luke states that Paul, on his second missionary journey, went from Neapolis to "Philippi, which is the leading city of the district of Macedonia, and a Roman colony" (Acts 16:12). If Luke states the facts accurately, we would expect the details of his statement to be in agreement with other historical facts about the city of Philippi in Macedonia.

Since the documents of the Bible are approximately 2,000 years old and older, their accuracy is tested by the science of archaeology. The word *archaeology* means "a study of ancient things." The examples given in this chapter are a brief description of some of the more significant contributions archaeology has made toward our understanding of the accuracy of Scripture.

We must approach the testimony of archaeology with caution. As significant as the contributions of archaeology are, we must understand that a certain archaeological discovery can, at best, *imply* that a biblical statement is accurate or inaccurate. For example, suppose that we find an ancient inscription which reads "Philippi of Macedonia is the *second* leading city." Would that discovery prove that Luke was in error in Acts 16:12? Not at all, because there is the possibility that the author of the inscription, rather than Luke, is inaccurate in his statement.

We must realize that it is futile to expect archaeology to prove that the entire Bible is true. But archaeological discovery has *tended* to support the historical claims of Scripture. Nelson Glueck, a well-known Jewish archaeologist, made the remarkable claim, "It may be stated categorically that no archaeological discovery has ever controverted a biblical reference."[1]

Archaeological Discovery
May Alter Bible Translations

Most of the differences in the versions of the Bible are the result of preferences of the translators. Frequently a translator will have several English words that correspond to the word to be translated from which to choose. Occasionally, archaeological discovery aids the translation process. For example, carefully compare the following translations from the *same Hebrew manuscript* text of 1 Samuel 1:24, 25:

American Standard Version, 1901	Revised Standard Version, 1952
And when she had weaned him, she took him up with her, with three bullocks, and one ephah of meal, and a bottle of wine, and brought him unto the house of Jehovah in Shiloh: and the child was young.	And when she had weaned him, she took him up with her, along with a three-year-old bull, an ephah of flour, and a skin of wine; and she brought him to the house of the Lord at Shiloh; and the child was young.
And they slew the bullock, and brought the child to Eli.	Then they slew the bull, and they brought the child to Eli.

The American Standard Version along with the King James Version states that Hannah brought *three bullocks* with her when she came to the house of the Lord at Shiloh to dedicate young Samuel to God. However, the text proceeds to state that she offered *one bullock*. The Revised Standard Version says that Hannah brought one three-year-old bullock for the dedication service and offered it. Did Hannah bring one bullock, or did she bring three bullocks? If she brought three bullocks, why did she offer just one? For many years this discrepancy was a mystery to the translators.

An archaeological discovery provided the answer. In the Hebrew text, words are not separated by spaces. The same text can be translated "three bullocks" or "a bullock of three." Both translations are correct. Subsequent to the 1901 American Standard Version, Near Eastern archaeologists excavating in Iraq discovered ancient Assyrian clay tablets that solved the mystery.[2] The archaeologists learned that, in referring to the age of an animal, writers understood but did not write the word "year". The phrase "bullock three" means "a bullock of three years." They concluded, then, that Hannah brought one three-year-old bullock and offered it to God. The 1952 Revised Standard Version translators used this information when they translated the Hebrew text. Most archaeological discoveries have confirmed the historical accuracy of Scripture.

A Bible Error Concerning a Whole Nation of People?

Before 1906 no historical information about the nation of the Hittites existed except that given in the Bible. Bible critics, therefore, concluded that the Hittite nation never existed and that biblical references to the Hittites were in error. Joshua claims that the Hittites lived in Canaan before it was occupied by Israel (Joshua 3:10). David's wife, Bathsheba, was said to have been married to Uriah the Hittite (2 Samuel 11:3). Were the Bible critics right? Was the Bible in error regarding a whole nation of people?

During 1906 and 1907, excavations in eastern Turkey revealed evidence of an extensive Hittite empire that had flourished during Bible times.[3] Life-sized reliefs of Hittite warriors carved out of black basalt were found. We now know that the Hittites were stocky people with prominent noses who wore heavy coats and turned-up-toe shoes. They wore their hair long over their shoulders, with high dented caps. Their short aprons were fastened with wide belts. The discovery of over 10,000 tablets from the ancient Hittite capital confirmed the claim of Joshua 1:4 that the ancient fertile crescent was the "land of the Hittites." The Bible was accurate concerning the Hittites, and the critics were wrong.

Did Moses Write the Law of Moses?

Before 1902, many critics claimed that Moses could not have written the Pentateuch: Genesis, Exodus, Leviticus, Numbers, and Deuteronomy. Their reasoning was that writing had not been invented by the time Moses led the Israelites from bondage under Pharaoh in Egypt. Hieroglyphics, or pictograph writing, was known from the pyramids of Egypt and elsewhere, but alphabet writing, called *cuneiform* writing, was *not* known. It is interesting how critics tend to assume that it is the Bible that is in error rather than themselves!

A "stele" is an ancient stone monument. In 1902 archaeologists discovered the magnificent black diorite stele which contains the Code of Hammurabi, King of Babylon, who lived several hundred years before Moses. This code contains 282 laws and is the longest ancient cuneiform writing known.[4] The discovery confirmed that alphabet writing was indeed known when Moses was supposed to have written the Pentateuch.

Critics, however, do not give up easily. Indeed, even after it had been confirmed that alphabet writing was known in Moses' day, the critics claimed that alphabet writing was not practiced by the Israelites. In 1929 a peasant was plowing in his field in North Syria about forty miles southwest of the biblical city of Antioch. His plow dug into something in the ground. His discovery was no less than fifty tablets written in an alphabet of a previously unknown language. Later, language dictionaries and lists of synonyms were also discovered. The writings dated to the 15th and 14th centuries B.C. and were written in very ancient Hebrew. They were called the Ras-shamra or Ugaritic documents.[5] The discovery made by the Syrian peasant forever silenced the claim that Moses could not have written the Pentateuch.

It is also of interest that the Ugaritic documents shed considerable light on the moral depravity of the Canaanites. This discovery helps us to understand the justice of God in commanding the Israelites to utterly destroy the cults of Canaan.

Did Isaiah Know What He Was Talking About?

For many years, critics thought that Isaiah made an error when he named Sargon as king of Assyria in Isaiah 20:1. They thought it was an error because Sargon is named in no other place in the Bible or secular writings. However, in 1843 at Khorsabad, near the ancient city of Nineveh, archaeologist Paul Emile Botta made a significant discovery that confirmed Isaiah's reference to Sargon.[6]

Botta unearthed Sargon's temple and even discovered an eight-foot high carved relief portrait of the bearded Sargon. The walls of his palaces were elaborately decorated with writings which revealed many records of his reign as king of Assyria—just as Isaiah claims. In 1963 fragments of a stele set up by the ancient Assyrians in the land of Ashdod were discovered, again confirming Isaiah's reference to Sargon, King of Assyria. Sargon is no longer a shadowy figure of ancient history.

A Missionary Helped the Archaeologist

In 2 Kings 1:1 we read about Mesha, King of Moab, who led a rebellion against Israel. In the rebellion, Elisha the prophet helped the kings of Israel, Judah, and Edom as they joined forces against the king of Moab. A terrible battle ensued, and, when Mesha saw that the battle was going against him, he offered his oldest son as a burnt offering to Chemosh, the god of the Moabites. The account in 2 Kings clearly shows that the king of Moab failed in his rebellion.

In 1868 a German missionary named Klein accidentally discovered the now famous Moabite, or Mesha, stone while visiting the ancient land of Moab.[7] The writings on this stone give Moab's account of the rebellion. The story on the stone agrees in many details with the biblical account, and several biblical towns are named on the stone. Mesha, King of Moab, claimed, however, that Chemosh had helped him gain a victory and boasted that "Israel has perished forever." It is not surprising that Mesha left a biased account of the battle in which he suffered a great and embarrassing loss.

Was Abraham an Ignorant Nomad?

During the 19th century, it was popular for Bible critics to doubt the historical accuracy of the story of Abraham found in Genesis 11 through 13. There we are told that Abraham lived in the land of Ur of the Chaldees in Mesopotamia. The Bible describes Abraham as a wealthy man with silver, gold, cattle, and herdsmen. Furthermore, we are told that Abraham traveled a great distance from Ur of the Chaldees to the land of Canaan. Bible critics claimed that if the Land of Ur of the Chaldees ever existed it was far too primitive for a person like Abraham.

Sir Charles Leonard Woolley, an Englishman, was a distinguished biblical archaeologist. During the period 1922-1934 Woolley did extensive archaeological work on the ancient city of Ur of the Chaldees.[8] His excavations led to the discovery that education was actually well developed in Ur at the time Abraham is supposed to have lived there. Students in Ur learned reading, writing, and arithmetic at the time of Abraham. Woolley's work also demonstrated that commerce was well developed. Ships came to

Ur from the Persian Gulf bringing copper ore, ivory, gold, and hardwoods. Once again, the spade of the archaeologists confirmed the claims of Scripture.

A Young Boy Makes a Discovery

In 1880 two Arab boys were playing by the Pool of Siloam in Jerusalem when one of them fell into the pool. Groping about in the pool, the boy discovered a tunnel passage which had long been forgotten. The passage was two feet wide and five feet high and reached 1,800 feet under the streets of Jerusalem from the Pool of Siloam to the Gihon Spring near Jerusalem.[9]

Ancient Hebrew writings were inscribed in the stone walls of the tunnel passageway. Experts deciphered the writing and determined that the tunnel was the conduit which King Hezekiah commissioned workers to build to bring water into Jerusalem from the spring outside the city. The record of Hezekiah's building the pool and the conduit is recorded in 2 Kings 20:20:

> The rest of the deeds of Hezekiah, and all his might, and how he made the pool and the conduit and brought water into the city, are they not written?

The deciphered writing on the inside of the tunnel tells the story of the boring of the tunnel through the limestone rock underneath Jerusalem hundreds of years before.

A Shepherd Boy
Makes the Greatest Discovery of All!

In the spring of 1947, a shepherd boy in search of his father's lost lambs tossed a stone into a shadowy cave. Hearing the sharp crack of shattered pottery, he was frightened and ran for assistance. The result was the discovery of the Dead Sea Scrolls. Distinguished archaeologist William F. Albright states that this discovery was "the most important discovery ever made in Old Testament manuscripts" (qtd. in Tenney).[10]

With the toss of a shepherd boy's stone, archaeologists spanned 1,000 years in a single discovery. The scrolls discovered in the clay jars of the Qumran caves are at least 1,000 years older than the best Old Testament manuscripts previously in our possession. The Dead Sea Scrolls contain the oldest known manuscript of the complete book of Isaiah and fragments of every book in the Old Testament except the book of Esther.

One cave alone contained 382 manuscripts, 100 of which were Bible manuscripts. The content of the biblical Dead Sea Scrolls has confirmed rather than challenged our confidence in the integrity of the Scriptures. Differences in the texts of the scrolls and the best previous Old Testament manuscripts are slight.[11]

Luke Was an Accurate Historian

Luke was not only a physician; he was a historian who wrote with meticulous detail. In Luke 2:1-3 he makes reference to the census which was taken at the time of the birth of Christ. He claims that the census was taken when Cyrenius was governor of Syria and that everyone had to go to his own city for enrollment.

Bible critics have accused Luke of three errors in this account. Their accusations have been that (a) the census did not occur at all, (b) Cyrenius was not governor at the time Luke said he was, and (c) everyone was not required to go to his ancestral city for enrollment.

But as J. P. Free points out, archaeological discovery has demonstrated that Luke was accurate in each of the details concerning the census.[12] Archaeologists have discovered a number of papyri documents that contain references to the census that was made about the time Luke indicates. Second, archaeological discovery has shown that Cyrenius served two terms as governor, confirming Luke's statement. Third, an edict dating back to 104 A.D. has been discovered and indicates that people were subject to census and were required to return to their ancestral homes just as Luke states.

History and Archaeology Confirm Prophecy

In Ezekiel 26 we find the following truly remarkable prophecy against Tyre, a Phoenician city on the coast of the Mediterranean. The specific details of this prophecy are highlighted.

> Therefore thus says the Lord God: Behold, I am against you O Tyre, and **will bring up many nations against you,** as the sea brings up its waves. **They shall destroy the walls of Tyre, and break down her towers;** and **I will scrape her soil from her, and make her a bare rock.** She shall be in the midst of the sea a place for the spreading of nets; for I have spoken, says the Lord God; and she shall become a spoil to the nations. They will make spoil of your riches and a prey of your merchandise; **they will break down your walls** and destroy your pleasant houses; **your stones and timber and soil they will cast into the midst of the waters.** And I will **stop the music of your songs, and the sound of your lyres shall be heard no more.** I will make you a bare rock; **you shall be a place for the spreading of nets; you shall never be rebuilt;** for I the Lord have spoken, says the Lord God. Ezekiel 26:3-6; 12-14

Ezekiel's remarkable prophecy against Tyre was not fulfilled for more than 250 years. Yet historians and archaeologists have confirmed the prophecy of Tyre's destruction just as Ezekiel predicted.[13]

Nebuchadnezzar, King of Babylon, brought a siege against Tyre which lasted for thirteen years. During the siege, the citizens of Tyre moved most of their possessions to a small island one-half mile offshore in the Mediterranean Sea. After Nebuchadnezzar's troops retreated, Tyre was left deserted and the old city became isolated. Her songs ceased, and her harps became silent. However, the walls and many of the buildings of the city remained intact. Two-hundred and forty years later Ezekiel's prophecy had not yet been fulfilled.

However, in 334 B.C., Alexander the Great, King of Macedonia, brought a second siege against the new city of Tyre on the off-shore island. Alexander made a causeway reaching to the island of new Tyre out of the timbers and ruins of old Tyre. The troops of Alexander the Great completely ravaged the little island, and fishermen spread their nets on the causeway to dry to this day. Tyre was never rebuilt.

Conclusion

The overwhelming evidence from historical and archaeological testimony confirms that *you can trust your Bible*. Through His Holy Spirit, God has Divinely inspired His message to man. By means unknown to us, God's word has been preserved. Christ gave us this promise: "Heaven and earth will pass away, but my words will not pass away" (Mark 13:31).

This is my Father's world,
And to my list'ning ears,
All nature sings, and round me rings,
The music of the spheres.

M. D. Babcock

12

Can A Modern Scientist Believe the Bible?

Can a modern scientist believe the Bible? The answer is an enthusiastic "YES!" Most early scientists believed in God and the Bible. Many outstanding modern scientists continue to do so. I am acquainted with many scientists who are Christians, some of whom have excelled in their chosen scientific fields in colleges, universities, and research institutions, and in industry as well.

Modern science and its resulting technology have highlighted rather than excluded the need for belief in God and the moral standards of Scripture. The threat of global nuclear war has created within most of us a desire to believe that a power greater than man is in control of the destiny of our planet.

Medical advances in recent years have raised scores of moral and ethical issues pertaining to such things as organ transplants, euthanasia, DNA recombination, genetic engineering, and *in vitro* fertilization. A society which rejects God and the moral standards of Scripture is likely to address these issues from a humanistic or materialistic perspective. Although many modern moral and ethical issues are not directly addressed by the Scriptures, it has never been more urgent for men and women of science to be aware of the moral standards of God's Word.

What Is Science?

Science is a human activity. God has given us nature, and God has given us human intellect, but He has not given us science. Science has its origin totally in man's attempt to understand and subdue nature.

A few years ago, my family and I went on a twenty-three-night camping trip to the West Coast. Standing on the rim of the Grand Canyon at sunset and later overlooking Yosemite Valley were unforgettable experiences that provoked us to worship the Creator. However, the Grand Canyon is not science. Yosemite Valley is not science. The Pacific Ocean is not science. Likewise, the beautiful fossil serving as a bookend on my shelf is not science. These things are observations, and observations are where science begins.

Science is not a body of static, established facts. Science is always changing; it is never constant. Scientists are always opening new doors. In the introduction to his textbook in human genetics, Curt Stern states, "The scientific literature is a veritable graveyard of discarded hypotheses."[1] He is correct, but this is not a criticism of science; the willingness to change is one of science's finest virtues.

No scientific hypothesis, theory, or law is sacred. Each of these, regardless of how fundamental it may be, is subject to revision as scientists discover new data or reinterpret old data. Although a good scientist is not capricious, he always has the prerogative of changing his mind. Scientific laws as fundamental as the Law of Conservation of Matter and Energy or the Law of Gravitation have been revised and re-revised since they were originally introduced. As we are soon to enter the 21st century, no one understands better than the scientist that we do not stand on the pinnacle of scientific knowledge. There is much more to discover.

We conclude, then, that science is an ever-changing activity of human intellect by which man attempts to understand nature. This definition of science, although not exhaustive, is the basis for our approach in the remainder of this chapter.

Scientists Rely on Faith

Many people do not understand that scientists rely on faith. The laws of thermodynamics are fundamental concepts in the natural sciences. However, these laws are not accepted because scientists have proved them to be true; they are accepted because no one has ever observed an exception to them. It is, in fact, impossible to *prove* the laws of thermodynamics because they speak of abstract and theoretical concepts such as the total energy content of the universe, absolute zero temperature, and perfectly ordered crystals.

The principle of gravitation has widespread implications within the sciences. We can write a mathematical equation which describes gravitation. Using our understanding of gravitation, we can engage in interplanetary space flight within our solar system and beyond. However, we do not understand *why* one physical body in the universe *should* intrinsically attract another physical body in the universe. Scientific investigation is generally limited to "what" and "how", but not "why", questions.

In mathematics, we start with definitions, axioms, and postulates which we do not attempt to prove. For example, we may state that parallel lines never meet. From this postulate, which has never been proved to be a true statement, Euclidean geometry develops. From the statement that parallel lines *do* meet, which has also never been proved, nonEuclidean geometry develops, giving rise to interesting systems such as curved space.

It is important for both scientists and nonscientists to understand that scientists rely on faith. The scientist who understands this fact is less likely to be critical of a person who professes religious faith. The religious person who understands it is less likely to be intimidated by the scientist.

Areas of Agreement Between Science and Scripture

The intention of the biblical writers was to present truth. It was not their intention to be "scientific." What is "scientific" changes with each generation, but Scripture is timeless. It is appropriate to expect the Bible to be accurate with respect to its intended message for any generation. However, it is *not* appropriate to expect the Bible to agree with all of the scientific views of any particular generation. Nevertheless, there are areas where Scripture and science are in complete agreement.

Among astrophysicists and cosmologists today, there is virtual agreement that the universe has not existed forever. Today's scientists who hold this view are in complete agreement with Scripture which declares that the universe is not eternal: "In the beginning God created the heavens and the earth" (Genesis 1:1).

Scripture sanctions the moral activities of scientists. Science itself is neither moral nor immoral; science is amoral. Every scientist, however, is a moral being, and in Genesis 1:28, God sanctions the moral activities of men when He says: "Have dominion over the fish of the sea and over the birds of the air, and over the cattle, and over all the earth, and over every living thing that moves upon the earth." Animal experiments are essential to the progress of science and, if properly conducted, are not immoral. Such experiments are impossible in animistic societies where animals are worshiped. Human experiments, however, such as those conducted by the Nazis in German concentration camps during World War II, are immoral. Such activity as this is condemned by Scripture. Science and technology have made their greatest strides in societies where Christian ideals of truth and pursuit of knowledge are honored.

I recently received a gift from one of my students who is talented in the art of calligraphy. On parchment he had beautifully penned one of my favorite Old Testament scriptures: "It is the glory of God to conceal things, but the glory of kings is to search things out" (Proverbs 25:2). Russian chemist Demitri Mendeleev is the father of the modern periodic chart of the chemical elements. It is claimed that Mendeleev's mother whispered the words of this proverb to her son as she was dying. The proverb could be the motto of every research scientist. Other than extracting and disseminating truth from God's revelation, the Bible, there is no higher honor for man than to extract truth from God's revelation, nature.

Areas of Disagreement Between Science and Faith

When I entered college as an eighteen-year-old Christian aspiring to major in the sciences, I was naive to expect that everything I would learn in science would support Christian faith. Many things I learned did reinforce faith, but I also encountered areas of disagreement. If we correctly understand the nature of both science and Christian faith, we will not be surprised that conflicts sometimes exist. However, these conflicts need not be disastrous to faith. The following diagram, adapted from my book, *Faith and Evidence*,[2] illustrates the origin of the conflict:

CONFLICT AND AGREEMENT IN SCIENCE AND FAITH

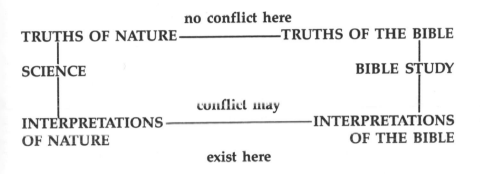

no conflict here

TRUTHS OF NATURE————————TRUTHS OF THE BIBLE

SCIENCE   BIBLE STUDY

conflict may

INTERPRETATIONS————————INTERPRETATIONS
OF NATURE   OF THE BIBLE

exist here

Conflict, when it exists, is not between the truths of nature and the truths of Scripture. Science is a process which leads to hypotheses, theories, and laws which are interpretations of nature. Bible study, likewise, leads to a variety of interpretations of God's Word. However, truth derived by a careful exercise of the scientific process does not conflict with truth obtained through diligent Bible study. Truth cannot conflict with truth. It is in the *interpretation* of nature *and* Scripture that conflict sometimes arises. The following are some reasons why misunderstandings lead to conflict.

(a) The Bible does not teach everything that many claim it teaches.

Many people who object to Scripture have not investigated to see if the Bible really teaches what they think it teaches. My biology professor in college gave his students a handout which had been prepared by a professor at another institution. It contained a list of objections to Genesis 1. Although I was a college freshman, I could see that the author of the paper did not understand the intent of Genesis 1. It is important to understand that Genesis 1 does not teach everything that everyone says it teaches!

The footnotes or margin notes of many Bibles cite the date for the creation of the world and Adam and Eve as 4004 B.C. This date was derived by Irish Bishop James Ussher, a contemporary of Shakespeare, 400 years ago. Ussher used the genealogical tables of the Bible to determine his date for creation. Lightfoot, a Hebrew scholar who was a contemporary of Ussher, further concluded that creation occurred during the week of October 18-24, 4004 B.C. with Adam's being created on October 23 at 9 a.m. 45th meridian time (Ramm).[3]

Although Ussher and Lightfoot had good intentions, they misused biblical chronology. The word "begat" does not always mean "the father of" as we generally suppose. Names are often omitted in the genealogical tables. Matthew, in his genealogy of the ancestors of Christ, omits the names of three Judean kings, Ahaziah, Joash, and Amaziah, when he calls Joram "the father of Uzziah" (Matthew 1:8). Actually Uzziah was the great- great-grandson of Joram. It is also an abuse of Scripture to use these omissions in the Scriptural genealogical tables to argue that man has been on earth for millions of years.

Some people believe that most of earth's geological features should be understood in view of the Great Flood of Genesis 6. Scripture clearly states that the flood occurred. The flood is just as much a fact of Scripture as the creation of Adam and Eve is. However, the Bible does not teach that one must interpret geological phenomena on the basis of the flood.

(b) Bible writers often describe things as they appear to be.

Bible writers often describe things as they appear to be and not as they actually are. For example, they speak of the sun "rising" and "setting" even though we know that the sun does not rise and set. The earth rotates on its axis, giving the appearance of the motion of the sun. We should not be critical of the biblical writers for using this kind of language. Modern meteorologists use the same language today. Many apparent conflicts between science and Scripture are eliminated by keeping in mind that biblical writers often describe things *as they appear to the observer.* Doing so is using a legitimate literary technique.

The Apostle Paul used the literary technique of describing things as they appear to be in 1 Corinthians 15:36 where he suggests that a seed planted in the ground must die before a new plant can be produced. Some critics say that this is a scientific inaccuracy because, biologically, the seed does not die. In germination, life is changed from a dormant state to an active state. What is Paul's intention here? He is not teaching about seed germination at all. He is drawing an analogy between what *appears* to occur in the germination of a seed and what actually happens in the death and resurrection of the Christian. In Paul's analogy, the transformation that will occur when the Christian is resurrected is compared to the change that occurs as a seed is transformed into a plant. There is no scientific inaccuracy here. To charge the Bible with inaccuracy is to treat Scripture unfairly.

Moses is sometimes accused of being inaccurate because he classified bats as birds in Leviticus 11:19. Today, bats are classified as mammals and not birds. Again, this is not an inaccuracy, for all taxonomical classifications are arbitrary and are subject to change as scientists see the need. Modern scientists could just as well call "all animals that fly" birds, as Moses apparently did.

(c) Miracles are not scientific inaccuracies.

Miracles are not scientific inaccuracies; miracles are *not* subject to scientific analysis. Science must forever remain silent on whether approximately 180 gallons of water were turned into wine in Cana of Galilee 2,000 years ago. The Apostle John and a crowd of witnesses claim that the miracle occurred, but it cannot be repeated for scientific scrutiny. Likewise, science must remain silent on whether Jesus fed 5,000 people with a few loaves, walked on water, or was raised from the dead. No miracle of the Bible constitutes an area of conflict between modern science and Scripture because the miracles of the Bible lie beyond the proper realm of scientific investigation.

(d) Bible writers sometimes describe nature poetically.

Scientific inaccuracies sometime appear to exist in Scripture because Bible writers frequently describe nature poetically. For example, Job 26 is poetical. In verse 11, Job, in reference to the

131

mountains, calls them "pillars of heaven." He says they "tremble, and are astounded at his [God's] rebuke." By calling the mountains "pillars of heaven," Job is not making an unscientific reference to an outmoded world view. Rather he is using a poetic device called a metaphor.

Job uses an interesting poetic expression in verse 7, "He [God] . . . hangs the earth upon nothing." Either this passage represents an excellent example of scientific forethought of thousands of years, or else Job here exclaims poetically that "nothing supports the earth but the power of God's word." In view of the poetic nature of this section, the latter is the more likely meaning of the expression.

(e) The Bible is not a book of science.

Although we expect the Bible to be accurate when its message is properly understood, it is important to recognize that the Bible is not a book of science. Remember that science is a purely human activity. The revelation of God's Word in the Bible was a Divine activity. Nevertheless, a person will occasionally say, "The Bible is my book of science." It is with some embarrassment that I remember making that statement myself as a much younger person just beginning my career in science. The statement reflected my lack of understanding of both science and Scripture.

It is a deterrent to faith that well-meaning but misinformed persons misapply certain Scriptures in an attempt to discover scientific forethought in the Bible. Remember, Scripture is timeless; science changes. One is likely to abuse Scripture if he tries to make it conform to the scientific pronouncements of any particular age. I am not denying that Scripture is accurate or inspired when I say that certain Scriptures should *not* be applied as some people have applied them. God's Word is holy and sacred, and *any* abuse should be avoided.

Frequently, the "scientific content" of Scripture disappears altogether when one reads the Bible with the desire to understand its *intended message*. Most abuse of this kind is the result of the reader's imposing a scientific message on Scripture. Upon approaching any passage of Scripture, one's only desire should be to discover the message intended by the inspired writer.

A passage that will illustrate this point is Isaiah 40:22: "It is he who sits above the circle of the earth." Well-meaning persons claim that Isaiah knew that the earth was spherical rather than flat 2,500 years before Columbus sailed. God certainly could have revealed that information to Isaiah. However, is that what Isaiah intended to convey by his statement? As we search for the intended message of Isaiah 40:22, we must be aware that not all circular objects are spherical. For example, a plate is round, but it is flat. Also, had it been Isaiah's desire to say "spherical," or "round but not flat," he certainly could have done so.

Careful study of the context of Isaiah 40:22 indicates that the intention of the passage is far more sublime than teaching us about the shape of the earth. Isaiah, in context, is speaking of the sovereignty of God. The style of the section is poetical. Isaiah, therefore, apparently uses the expression "circle of the earth" in reference to the circle of the horizon as he expresses the sublime thought that "God is the Sovereign Lord of the whole earth." No scientific forethought is likely intended by the passage.

Frequently claims of scientific forethought disappear altogether when the student of the Bible consults other translations. For example, in Job 38:22 God asks Job, "Hast thou entered into the treasures of the snow?" (*KJV*). Well-meaning persons have offered several explanations of the treasures of snow in an effort to show that the Bible is inspired because it contains scientifically advanced information. "Treasures" have been identified as (a) fertilizer trapped in snow crystals, (b) gold trapped in snow crystals, (c) the snowflake symmetry, and (d) the slow manner in which snow melts to nourish the soil.

Upon consulting other translations, one will find that the apparent scientific forethought of Job 38:22 disappears altogether. "Treasures" is translated "treasuries" in the *ASV* and "storehouses" in the *RSV* and *NIV* translations. God is asking Job if he knows where snow comes from. Looking for scientific forethought in Scripture usually removes the reader's attention from the real intended message of Scripture. It is unfortunate that Job 38 has been so abused.

Many other examples of abuses of Scripture because of supposed scientific forethought could be listed here. However, these two examples should suffice. The reader is referred to my earlier book, *Faith and Evidence* if he would like an even more detailed treatment of the interpretation of nature passages in the Bible.[4]

The Scientific Silence of Scripture

The remarkable thing about Scripture is not that it contains scientific forethought but that it is virtually silent on scientific matters. Throughout the ages Scripture has declared that the power that sustains the world is God's Word. In contrast, the Chaldeans, who are frequently mentioned in the Old Testament, believed that the universe was an enclosed region supported by a sea in which the earth floated. They believed that the sky was a great vaulted dome made from hard metal that reflected light. Biblical writers, although doubtless familiar with this concept, did not speak of the earth in this way. In fact, it is doubtful that any particular scientific world view is presented in the Bible.

Ancient Egyptians believed the world was a large rectangular box. The length of the box represented north to south, and the width represented east to west. The bottom of the box was the earth, and Egypt was the center of the earth. The sky, according to the Egyptians, was supported by four high mountains. Moses was highly educated in all of the ways of the Egyptians (Acts 7:22) and was doubtless aware of this belief. Yet Genesis 1, which we believe was written by Moses, contains no reference to such an erroneous world view.

Ancient Hindu people believed the world floated on the back of a huge turtle which swam in an ocean of milk. Four elephants standing on the back of the turtle supported the earth. Everything was contained within the coils of a giant cobra. The Bible does not contain erroneous "science" such as this either.

The *Ebers Papyrus*, an Egyptian medical document contemporary with the period when the Israelites were held captive in Egypt, recommended many bizarre medical concoctions. Medications were made from such things as hippopotamus fat, a donkey's hoof, and worms' heads. Topical applications and teas were made from excreta of donkeys, antelopes, dogs, cats, flies, and human beings. These "treatments" were more likely to spread disease than to cure it. Moses was surely aware of these practices. Had the Bible been written by human impulse alone, "magical cures" such as these would surely have found their way into Scripture. We can be thankful that the Bible does not contain the "best science of its day."

Science Can Neither Prove nor Disprove the Bible

The nonscientist is often overly confident in the ability of science to prove or disprove claims. Unfortunately, with a fair degree of regularity certain stories circulate about scientists who are busy proving that the Bible is true. An example is the fictitious story of how NASA scientists discovered "indisputable computer evidence" of the lost day of Joshua 10 and thus proved the inspiration of the Bible. Although this story has been exposed numerous times as a hoax, it continues to circulate. The story resulted from the overactive imagination of a newspaper columnist. The eagerness with which stories like this are accepted reflects our unfortunate tendency to want to walk by sight rather than by faith.

In Chapter 11 we showed that the science of archaeology is one of our finest tools for certifying the accuracy of certain statements of Scripture. We also pointed out that it is not possible for archaeology to prove that the Bible is inspired or that it is accurate in every detail. Archaeology illuminates, but it does not prove, the Bible. Likewise, science may illuminate God's word, but it cannot prove the truth or inspiration of the Bible. If we will recall that science is *relative* and *changing*, we will appreciate the fact that it is hazardous to use science to prove Scripture which is *absolute* and *unchanging*.

Conclusion

Science is a legitimate career for a young Christian and is not necessarily hazardous to faith. However, due to the dynamic nature of science and the variety of interpretations placed on Scripture, one should not be surprised to encounter conflict. The truths of nature do not conflict with the truths of God's Word. There must always be perfect harmony within truth. Science is a rational process and Christianity is a rational religion. Not only can a modern scientist be a Christian; many modern scientists *are* Christians. Most fortunate among scientists are those who interpret reality through the eyes of the creator and sustainer of the universe, Jesus Christ.

O Lord my God! When I in awesome wonder
Consider all the worlds Thy hands have made,
I see the stars, I hear the rolling thunder,
Thy pow'r throughout the universe displayed.

Carl Boberg

13

Can A Modern Scientist Believe Genesis One?

In the overall scheme of things, the greatest of all questions is *not* "Can I believe Genesis 1?" The greatest of all questions is *"God, are you really there?"* If the answer to that question is "yes," then all other questions about subjects revealed in the Bible—such as the creation of man, the virgin birth, miracles, the resurrection of Christ, and life hereafter—are relatively small questions.

A person who acknowledges God's existence will have no major difficulty accepting Genesis 1. When I refer to Genesis 1, I refer to *exactly what Genesis 1 says*, not to what scores, and even hundreds, of biblical interpreters claim it says. Extensive treatises and theories on Genesis 1 are interesting, but unnecessary, to one who has made a commitment to believe in God. Remember, the Bible does not teach everything that everyone says it teaches.

Genesis 1 is a factual, but not exhaustive, account of the miracle of creation. Like the rest of the Bible, it is not written in the scientific language of any age. Suppose God had intended to describe creation "scientifically." Would he have chosen the language of Aristotle, Galileo, Newton, Einstein, or some scientist to be born centuries later? Although the Genesis record is an accurate account of Divine creation, it is not a scientific account. Genesis 1 is as timeless in its message as the rest of the Bible is.

The New Testament on Genesis One

A compelling reason for a Christian to believe Genesis 1 is that Christ and the New Testament writers accepted it as a factual and historical account of creation. Christ, the agent of creation (John 1:1, 3, 14), teaches that God made man and woman in the beginning (Mark 10:6). The Apostle Paul affirms the creative activity of God in and through Christ (Romans 1:19, 20; Colossians 1:16). By faith, Christians are to understand that the world was created by the Word of God (Hebrews 11:1, 3).

A clear statement that creation was the result of God's command is 2 Corinthians 4:6: "For it is the God, who said, 'Let light shine out of darkness.'" Paul states in his Athenian sermon that "God . . . made the world and everything in it" (Acts 17:24). It is notable that the biblical writers make no reference to *how* God created or *when* God created. Christians should accept Genesis 1 on the same basis that Christ and the New Testament writers accepted it, the basis of faith. Christian faith does not require that one understand the process God used or know the time when He created the universe and life on earth.

Genesis One and Modern Science

Christians should *not* attempt to harmonize the Genesis record with modern science. Today's science is in its infancy in its efforts to answer questions about the origin of the universe and life on earth. Indeed, it is impossible for scientific investigation ever to produce definitive answers to these questions. The changing nature of science prevents any realistic hope that Genesis 1 will ever be harmonized with modern science. By this I do not mean that Genesis 1 is inaccurate. However, I do mean that harmony should not be expected until science has identified *truth* relative to origins. That is not likely to happen.

Scientific investigation will continue on the problem of origins, and, in the future, there will be no lack of theories. If the world stands, a hundred years from now, scientists will still be introducing theories on origins. The Christian position, however, will remain unchanged: "By faith we understand that the world was created

138

by the Word of God" (Hebrews 11:3).

Let me illustrate what I mean about not attempting to harmonize science with the Genesis record. I am frequently asked, "How do you harmonize the existence of the dinosaurs with Genesis?" To this question, I respond, "I do not try." However, if God included the dinosaurs among the "great sea monsters," "living creatures," "beasts of the earth," and "creeping things" of days five and six in Genesis 1 that is fine with me. God has chosen not to elaborate on the details of creation.

Many attempts have been made to harmonize Genesis 1 with science. Consequently, numerous theories on the interpretation of Genesis 1 have resulted. However, I know of no attempt to harmonize Genesis 1 with science that has been successful.

The Alternative to Genesis One Is Unacceptable

The most widely accepted alternative to creation is materialistic evolution. This is a complex subject, and it is not appropriate to address it in detail here. However, brief summaries of the two important phases of materialistic evolution are presented. The two phases are (a) the chemical evolution of life and (b) the biological evolution of life.

(a) The Chemical Evolution of Life

Modern science now agrees with the Bible that life has not existed on earth forever. Beyond this, there is little agreement between the claims of Scripture and the claims of science on the origin of life. There appear to be only three alternatives to explain life on earth. They are (a) God created life on earth; (b) life came to earth from elsewhere in the universe; (c) a spontaneous generation of life occurred. The first alternative is the claim of Scripture. The second alternative, that life came to earth from outer space, is called *panspermia*, which shifts the problem of the origin of life from this planet to elsewhere in the universe. The third theory, spontaneous generation, is the alternative preferred by modern materialists and is discussed below.

More than 200 years ago, many people believed in a theory of spontaneous generation of life which has long since been discarded.

That theory supposed that life arose from rotting meat, decaying logs, and barnyard manure and was disproved by Louis Pasteur in 1864. For most of the next two centuries, spontaneous generation was regarded as superstition while the biblical principle "all life from life" prevailed. Now, largely due to the work of Russian biochemist A. I. Oparin and English biochemist J. B. S. Haldane, a new theory of spontaneous generation is held by materialistic scientists and philosophers.

The new theory claims that molecular collisions alone were responsible for a process now called chemical evolution. It claims that gradually the process caused matter to increase in complexity until finally matter took on new properties which we call "life." The theory denies any supernatural influence. It can be represented as follows:

SPONTANEOUS GENERATION OF LIFE

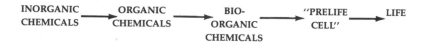

Some scientists estimate that more than a billion years may have been required for the process to have occurred. The word "spontaneous" does not mean "instantaneous." Rather it means that only forces within matter were responsible for the origin of life. The probability that such an event occurred, even once, is virtually zero.[1] However, the reverse of the process, the decomposition of life, is highly probable. Harvard University Nobel Prize winner George Wald claims that a modern scientist has no choice but to suppose that life arose by spontaneous generation:

> I think a scientist has no choice but to approach the origin of life through a hypothesis of spontaneous generation.

However, Wald also acknowledges the practical impossibility of the process:

140

One has only to contemplate the magnitude of this task to concede that the spontaneous generation of a living organism is impossible. Yet here we are—as a result, I believe, of spontaneous generation.[2]

The reason an intelligent scientist, such as Wald, can make such a statement is easy to understand. If a person believes that matter alone exists, the only option is quite clear: life has spontaneously arisen from nonlife because we are here. *The impossible must have occurred.* One who believes the biblical record, however, is not forced to such an awkward conclusion. He acknowledges that God created matter and subsequently produced life.

The practical impossibility of a spontaneous generation of life on earth's sterile and hostile surface is seen by examining the complexity of the "prelife cell" in the above scheme. Rocks, amino acids, proteins, complex molecules, and even viruses *are not alive.* The simplest living cells on this planet are bacteria, but there are simple and complex bacteria. *Escherichia coli* is one of the complex bacteria. It is a single-cell organism, and, it is estimated that it contains about 5,000 different kinds of chemical compounds. Among these compounds are an estimated 3,000 different kinds of proteins and 1,000 different kinds of nucleic acids.[3]

Scientists agree that the "prelife cell" would have been much less complex than an *E. coli* cell. Single-cell organisms less complex than *E. coli* are bacteria-like organisms called "mycoplasmas," which maintain their existence through a parasitic relationship with other cells. Biophysicists think that the "prelife cell" in the above scheme could possibly have been one-half as complex as a mycoplasma. However, according to biochemists and biophysicists, it would still have possessed a staggering complexity:

A cell of this size would have, in its non-aqueous substance, about 1.5 million atoms. Combined in groups of about 20 each, these atoms would form 75,000 amino acids and nucleotides, the building blocks from which the large molecules of the cell's metabolic and reproductive apparatus would be composed. Since these large molecules each incorporate about 500 building blocks, the cell would have a complement of 150 large molecules. This purely theoretical cell would be delicate in the extreme, its ability to reproduce successfully always threatened by the random thermal motion of its constituents.[4]

We should observe that the hypothetical cell just described is *far simpler than any form of life known to exist on earth*. It represents the theoretical lowest limit of complexity of life. Yet it is utterly complex. Except to the most persistent materialist, it is inconceivable that chance alone could have slowly and spontaneously constructed such a cell. Faith in Divine creation is certainly no more incredible than faith in matter!

The materialist sometimes makes the following faith statement: "One has only to wait: time itself performs miracles."[5] This is a gross overstatement. The fact is that time does nothing in and of itself. Even if the earth is billions of years old, that is not enough time for even the simplest life form to spontaneously evolve. *Life did not evolve; life was created.*

(b) The Biological Evolution of Life

We must recognize that biological evolution is a complex subject. Although some aspects of evolution theory are best described as a faith of the materialists, aspects of the theory which can be demonstrated include: *microevolution, adaptation,* and *speciation.* Microevolution and adaptation are observable processes that lead to the formation of new species, called speciation. Speciation may be represented as follows:

SPECIATION

SPECIES "B"

SPECIES "A"   **SPECIES "C"**

SPECIES "D"

The fact that scientists have cataloged no less than 250,000 species of beetles alone is evidence that the process of speciation occurs. Mutation rates that result in speciation are statistically predictable. The Christian should not deny that this kind of biological change takes place. New viruses are constantly being formed, and scientists are developing hybrid forms of plants and animals. This evidence testifies to the observable fact of microevolution, adaptation, and speciation.

Proponents of spontaneous generation believe that the original life cells were algae-like fermenting cells. They further suppose that biological evolution of life took over after chemical evolution produced life. The theory that all plants and animals, including man, have evolved from nonliving chemicals on earth's early surface is called *general evolution* distinguishable from *microevolution*. Microevolution, adaptation and speciation are observable as processes; general evolution is *not* observable as a process. It is furthermore unwarranted to conclude that general evolution occurred through the process of speciation. General evolution is represented by the following diagram:

GENERAL EVOLUTION

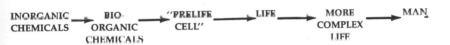

INORGANIC CHEMICALS → BIO-ORGANIC CHEMICALS → "PRELIFE CELL" → LIFE → MORE COMPLEX LIFE → MAN

Evidence that *general evolution* of higher living forms, such as man, occurred from lower living forms, such as prelife cells, is lacking. G. A. Kerkut, an evolutionist, identifies seven assumptions of the general theory of evolution. The first two assumptions pertain to the origin of life, and the remaining five pertain to the subsequent biological evolution of life. Kerkut's seven assumptions of general evolution theory are:

1. Nonliving things gave rise to living, i.e. spontaneous generation occurred.

2. Spontaneous generation of life occurred only once.

3. Viruses, bacteria, plants, and animals are interrelated.

4. The Protozoa gave rise to the Metazoa.

5. The invertebrate phyla are interrelated.

143

6.   The invertebrates gave rise to the vertebrates.

7.   Within the vertebrates the fish gave rise to the amphibia, the amphibia gave rise to the reptiles, and the reptiles gave rise to the birds and mammals.

Kerkut makes the following comment on the assumptions of general evolution theory:

> The first point that I should like to make is that these seven assumptions by their nature are not capable of experimental verification. They assume that a certain series of events has occurred in the past. Thus though it may be possible to mimic some of these events under present- day conditions, this does not mean that these events must therefore have taken place in the past. All that it shows is that it is *possible* for such a change to take place.[6].

Kerkut correctly observes that the evolution of all living forms from nonliving matter is not subject to experimental verification. The fossil record does not support the conclusion that all life evolved from lower living forms. Rather the fossil record suggests that major living forms developed independently of one another. Scientific evidence, fossil or otherwise, which implies relationships among living organisms does not necessarily imply that one form is the ancestor of another. Relationships among living forms may imply a common Designer and Creator.

Specialists in human evolution continue to believe that man and the primates have a common ancestor. However, the evidence that scientists have accumulated over the last few years has weakened, and not strengthened, the supposed link between man and ape-like creatures of the distant past. Artists typically portray human evolution by showing man gradually evolving from a creature who walked on all fours to man who stands erect. According to Weaver, the best evidence that experts in human evolution have accumulated to date leads to the conclusion that *man's ancestors have always stood erect.*[7] Human evolutionists have not succeeded in linking man with the primates.

Theistic Evolution

Theistic evolution is sometimes offered as a compromise between materialistic evolution and the Genesis record. There are probably as many different views of theistic evolution as there are persons professing it. The theistic evolutionist generally supposes that God created natural laws and somehow guided general evolution along. As animal organisms evolved from a single, original cell, God is supposed to have created man's spirit and placed it into the body of a beast, at which time man became "a living soul." Although many persons accept theistic evolution, it is an unnecessary compromise for the Christian.

Inserting God into the scheme of general evolution makes it less appealing to materialists. God is a compromise they are unwilling to accept. Any concept of Divine intervention is incompatible with the faith of the materialist.[8]

Accepting a concept of theistic evolution does not make the Christian scientist a better scientist. I certainly would not presume to speak for my fellow Christians who are scientists. However, I personally do not find the evidence for general evolution convincing and, therefore, find theistic evolution to be an unnecessary compromise. I have accepted God's miraculous intervention in the miracles and the resurrection of Jesus Christ. I do not find it difficult to accept God's miraculous intervention in creation.

If theistic evolution is accepted, the question arises whether God has merely created natural law or intervened throughout the course of evolution to prod matter along. Neither alternative would seem to be preferred over the claim of Genesis that God created the universe, plant life, marine life, land life, and man. I do not know how God created anything any more than I know how Christ turned water into wine. However, we do not have to know; *we walk by faith and not by sight.*

Conclusion

Scripture claims that "In the beginning, God created the heavens and the earth" (Genesis 1:1). It also teaches that man was uniquely created in the image of God. In our modern age of enlightened science and technology, there is no reason why a scientist should not accept the claims of Scripture—including the Genesis record.

Christianity is rational because it rests on a solid foundation of supporting evidence. The principal evidence is Christ Himself, who alone is the focus of our faith. As we focus our eye of faith on Christ, we walk by faith and not by sight, and we trust in God who keeps His promises. Eventually, faith will be made sight: "When He appears we shall be like him, for we shall see him as he is" (1 John 3:2).

Endnotes

Chapter 2: How Should I Respond to Doubt?

[1] Lewis, C. S. *The Case for Christianity.* NY: Macmillan and Co., 1962, p. 45.

[2] Russell, B. *Why I Am Not a Christian.* NY: Simon and Schuster, 1957.

Chapter 3: Does Faith in God Make Sense?

[1] Wald, G. "Cosmology of Life and Mind," *Los Alamos Science,* 16, (1988): 11.

[2]Ibid.

Chapter 6: Why Must the Innocent Suffer?

[1] *Parade Magazine,* Jan. 19, 1986, p. 4.

[2] Ibid.

Chapter 7: Was Jesus Really a Man?

[1] Josephus, F. *Antiquities.*

[2] Bruce, F. F. *Jesus and Christian Origins Outside the New Testament.* Grand Rapids: Wm. B. Eerdmans, 1974, p. 21.

[3] Ibid.

[4] Ibid.

[5] Bruce, F. F. *The New Testament Documents: Are They Reliable?* Grand Rapids: Wm. B. Eerdmans, 1960, p. 113.

[6] Ibid.

[7] Tacitus, C. *Annals in Encyclopedia Britannica.* 1952, p. 168.

[8] *Pliny's Letter XCIV*, Trans. by Hutchinson, p. 403.

[9] Tenney, M. C. *New Testament Survey.* Grand Rapids: Wm. B. Eerdmans, 1961, p. 201.

[10] Durant, W. *Caesar and Christ.* NY: Simon and Schuster, 1944, p. 557.

Chapter 8: Is Jesus Really the Son of God?

[1]. Lewis, C. S. *The Case for Christianity.* NY: Mcmillan and Co., 1962, p. 45.

Chapter 9: Is God Silent?

[1] Theissen, H. C. *Introduction to the New Testament.* Grand Rapids: Wm. B. Eerdmans, 1944, p. 86.

[2] Barclay, W. *The Mind of Christ.* NY: Harper and Row, 1961, p. 248.

Chapter 10: Is the Bible God's Word?

[1] Moseley, M. E., and C. J. Mackey. "Chan Chan, Peru's Ancient City of Kings." *National Geographic* 143, No. 3 (March 1973): pp. 318-345.

[2] McIntyre, L. *The Incredible Incas and Their Timeless Land.* Washington, D. C.: National Geographic Society, 1975, p. 78.

³ Lewis, J. P. "The Transmission of the Texts of the Bible." *1962 Harding College Lectures*. Austin: Firm Foundation, 1962, p. 49.

⁴ Lightfoot, J. B. "The letter of the Smyrnaeans on the Martyrdom of S. Polycarp," paragraph 9. *The Apostolic Fathers*. Grand Rapids: Baker Book House, 1965.

⁵ Durant, W. *Caesar and Christ*. NY: Simon and Schuster, 1944, p. 557.

Chapter 11: Can I Trust My Bible?

¹ Glueck, N. *Rivers in the Desert*. NY: Straus and Giroux, 1959, p. 31.

² Tenney, M. C. *Pictorial Bible Dictionary*. Grand Rapids: Zondervan, 1967, p. 58.

³ Garstang, J. *The Land of the Hittites*. London: Constable and Co., 1910.

⁴ Pfeiffer, C. F. *The Biblical World*. Grand Rapids: 1966, pp. 276-280.

⁵ Pfeiffer, C. F. *The Biblical World*. Grand Rapids: 1966, pp. 591-596.

⁶ Lewis, J. P. *Biblical Backgrounds of Bible History*. Grand Rapids: Baker Book House, 1971, p. 40.

⁷ Kenyon, F. *The Bible and Archaeology*. NY: Harper and Bros., p. 166.

⁸ Wooley, C. L. *Ur of the Chaldees*. NY: Scribner's, 1930.

⁹ Free, J. P. *Archaeology and Bible History*. Wheaton, Ill: Van Kampen Press, 1950, p. 211.

¹⁰Tenney, M. C. *Pictorial Bible Dictionary*. Grand Rapids: Zondervan, 1967, p. 205.

[11] Schultz, S. J. *The Old Testament Speaks*. San Francisco: Harper and Row, 1980, p. 3.

[12] Free, J. P. *Archaeology and Bible History*. Wheaton, Il: Scripture Press, 1969, pp. 285-286. Pub. Inc., Wheaton, Ill., 1969, p. 285, 286.

[13] Lewis, J. P. *Biblical Backgrounds of Bible History*. Grand Rapids: Baker Book House, 1971, pp. 31, 51, 52, 79, 84, 131; Everest, H. W. *The Divine Demonstration*. St. Louis: Christian Pub. Co., 1884, pp. 292, 293.

Chapter 12: Can A Modern Scientist Believe the Bible?

[1] Stern, C. *Principles of Human Genetics*. W. H. Freeman, 2nd ed., 1960.

[2] England, D. *Faith and Evidence*. Delight, Ark.: Gospel Light Publishing Company, 1983, p. 118.

[3] Ramm, B. *The Christin View of Science and Scripture*. Grand Rapids: Wm. B. Eerdmans Pub. Co., 1956, p. 174.

[4] England, D. *Faith and Evidence*. Delight, Ark.: Gospel Light Publishing Co., 1983.

Chapter 13: Can A Modern Scientist Believe Genesis One?

[1] England, D. *A Christian View of Origins*. Grand Rapids: Baker Book House, 1972.

[2] Wald, G. "The Origin of Life," *The Molecular Basis of Life*. San Francisco: Freeman, edited by Haynes, R. H. and Hanawalt, P. C., p. 339.

[3] Lehninger, A. L. *Biochemistry,* 2nd ed. NY: Worth Publishers, 1975, p. 5.

[4] Morowitz, H., and M. Tourtellotte. "The Smallest Living Cells," *Scientific American* 206, No. 3 (March 1962): p. 117.

[5] Wald, G. "The Origin of Life," *The Molecular Basis of Life,* p. 6.

[6] Kerkut, G. A. *Implications of Evolution.* Pergamon Press, 1960, pp. 6, 7.

[7] Weaver, K. "The Search for Our Ancestors," *National Geographic* 168, No. 5 (Nov. 1985): p. 560.

[8] Bennetta, W. J. "Scientists Decry a Slick New Packaging of Creationism," *The Science Teacher Today.* May 1987, pp. 36-43.